What Readers Are Saying About
AFTER THE CALL

"This book perfectly illustrates God's love and intentional purpose for our lives. PLEASE READ THE BOOK!"

"Author Ruth Griffin has produced... a captivating book that answers the questions we all have: Why am I here and what is my purpose? Though many Christians know about Moses, Griffin will make his life come alive in a vibrant perspective. In an excellent writing style, Ruth Griffin [weaves] Moses' life and her personal experiences, along with biblical principles to produce this work that well deserves a five-star rating."

"Ruth Griffin is a gifted writer, but what amazes me with 'After The Call' is how effortlessly she illustrates the God-intended communion of all things human and divine. She captures the 'unimaginable' that occurs when our frailty embraces God's plan. Ms. Griffin shows us that WE ARE ALL candidates for God's grace and unstoppable PURPOSE."

Other Books By The Author

Speak Tenderly To Her

Stay With Me

Stepmother's Anonymous

The Book of Joy

AFTER THE CALL

Ruth E. Griffin

Studio Griffin
A Publishing Company
www.studiogriffin.net

After The Call. Copyright © 2011 Ruth E. Griffin

All Rights Reserved. Printed in the United States of America. No part of this book may be used or reproduced in any manner whatsoever without written permission except in the case of brief quotations embodied in critical articles and reviews.

For information, contact:
Studio Griffin
A Publishing Company
studiogriffin@outlook.com
www.studiogriffin.net

Unless otherwise indicated, all Scripture taken from The Amplified Bible, Copyright 1954, 1958, 1962, 1964, 1965, 1987, by the Lockman Foundation. All rights reserved. Used by permission.

Scripture quotations marked NIV are taken from the Holy Bible, New International Version®. Copyright © 1973, 1978, 1984 International Bible Society. Used by permission of Zondervan. All rights reserved.

The "NIV" and "New International Version" trademarks are registered in the United States Patent and Trademark Office by International Bible Society. Use of either trademark requires the permission of International Bible Society.

Cover Design by Ruth E. Griffin

Image by © Kevin Carden /Adobe

First Edition

ISBN-13: 978-1-7351353-0-4

1 2 3 4 5 6 7 8 9 10

For my family

Chapter 1
INTRODUCTIONS

As a toddler, I ran into the corner of a coffee table and broke open the skin above my left eyebrow. The wound was small, but deep enough to require stitches and leave me with a one-inch scar. Besides the scar though, I now boast a prudent awareness [or neurosis, depending on your point of view] of tables and children. Don't run inside, I am constantly yelling at my youngest as she does cartwheels in the living room. Be careful, I tell her as she sprints through the house. You see, once a wound heals and becomes a scar, it has the potential of strengthening us to strengthen others. The "wounding" experience obligates us to prevent, educate, help, and minister to others who find themselves in similar situations.

> *Simon, Simon, (Peter, listen) Satan has asked excessively that [all of] you be given up to him...but I have prayed especially for you...and when you yourself have turned again, strengthen and establish your brethren. (Luke 22.31-32)*

Peter denied Jesus in the moment of his

greatest need and this experience left him wounded enough to return to his former life [John 21]. However, once the wound healed, it turned him around and created in him a responsibility to share the gospel of God's love (the same love that received him back even after he denied Jesus) with those who would listen, regardless of their ethnicity or background.

The scar above my eyebrow is just one of many scars that I have; some are noticeable, others are not. Like Peter, though they have created in me that same sense of urgency to minister to others experiencing the same things I have; or as a preventive measure, to deter others from walking the same paths I have walked. I have been turned around to strengthen my "brethren". God alone qualifies us to minister, but it is those scars we bear that become our credentials when we are placed in a certain area of ministry or help.

The book you are about to read was born from the burden that's been placed on my heart to share how my life has been transformed and how yours can be as well. Though I understand my purpose and know what my destiny is now, it has not always been that way. I grew up in a Christian household and was raised in church, but I didn't know the value of my life. I mean, I knew I was here for a reason, but I didn't know what that reason was. I knew I had a destiny before me, but I didn't know how to connect my present with my future. I had no purpose, no focus, and no direction. I wasn't living my life, I was just existing.

Without direction, I had nowhere to go and I was going there fast. I was graduating art school with a newborn son and no significant other. I had no job, no place to live and no family to rely on. I didn't just hit rock bottom, I came crashing down. There was nothing I could do at that point but call on God. And there, in the midst of my own personal hell, God found me, purposeless and lost. He changed the direction of my life and set me on a course towards fulfilling my destiny, writing my story, and sharing it with others.

How does your story start? Or perhaps the better question is, do you know where your story will end? This is the burden on my heart and the basis of my book—helping you to walk into your destiny. Many fine books have been written on the subject of discovering your purpose and destiny, but what we need to know now is what to do once we do know.

We need to know what to do after God calls. Moses faced that same challenge after living eighty years of his life on his own terms. He had lived an extraordinary life by any measure, but this quickly changed when he committed murder and was forced into exile. He lost everything, including his identity. Then he came face to face with a burning bush that didn't burn and a God who wasn't ready to give up on him yet. Moses still had a destiny to fulfill and had to find a way to connect the life he was living to the one God was calling him to.

The Bible offers other examples of people like Moses, who had to confront their doubts, fears and past in order to hear God and move into their future. Jacob and Dinah chased after wealth and security outside of God's will and gained a lifetime of pain in the process. Mephibosheth and Joshua lost their destinies and recovered them by God's grace. Hatshepsut and Jochebed sacrificed their lives for a child who would change the world. By examining their lives through Moses' discourse with God in Exodus 3, we will be able to learn what it means to be called of God and how to begin walking into our destinies.

All of us have different beginnings, but our common ground is found in what we do after God calls. At some point, like Moses, we will all have to face our doubts, fears and past. Will you let them propel you into your future? I can't say that if you do what I did you will have the same results, but I can most assuredly say that if you seek the same God I did, you will find not just your destiny, but the path towards it.

Chapter 2
FOUNDATION

A friend of mine bought her first home recently, a modular house, factory manufactured and stocked full of amenities. From the garden tub to the brand-new appliances to the stained-glass windows and the spacious walk-in closets, this house was designed for luxury. However, all of it was useless to her as long as the house was not anchored to a plot of land. With no foundation, it was devoid of the purpose it was designed to serve.

Many of us are like that house, filled with our own amenities—talents, education, gifts, and beauty. We are a model of creation, yet with no ground to stand on, we wander about asking why we exist. We question our identities and our purpose never realizing our lives were made to accomplish more than many of us ever do. And like that house, we need a foundation.

Nothing about us is accidental. We did not evolve, nor did we just appear. We were created from a divine blueprint, formed in the image of God. We were born out of the consciousness of God, sculpted from the plans in his heart. We were made to reflect his glory. We were created to be his crowning joy.

> *So God created man in his own image. In the image and likeness of God he created him: male and female he created them. (Genesis 1.27)*

Like many of us today, God wanted a family to delight in, sons and daughter who would look up to him and call him, "father." He created man in his image and placed him in a garden called Eden, or delight. There in the garden of delight, man and woman lacked for nothing. They had provision, relationship, and the companionship of their creator. All this was procured for them; and when the day's work was done, they spent their evenings walking in the cool of the day with their God. This was God's original design: God delighting in us and us delighting in him.

Yet this garden was not paradise and the first son and daughter would sin, as we so often do. They would disobey God and because God could not delight in their disobedience, they were forced to leave Eden. However, while they were taken out of Eden, out of God's delight, Eden was not taken out of them. As their descendants, we still have God's design written on our hearts, but until we are living in that design, we will merely exist, void of direction and purpose.

Ah, but therein lies our purpose: it wasn't for our sake that God created Eden but for his. God's design was for a family to delight in, sons and daughters to spend his affection on, so that we in turn could delight in him, our heavenly father. We marred the plans with sin, thereby separating ourselves from God, but because of his great love for us, he made a way to reconcile us to him and bring us back to Eden. The atoning sacrifice Jesus Christ made on the cross. When we acknowledge Jesus as the only avenue back to God, then we are immediately welcomed back into his waiting arms. Some of us come to that knowledge early in life, some before their final breath and some not at all. It is for those children, the ones who do not know him, that God's heart beats for. The alternative to him is unthinkable, eternal separation from the children he loves. So when we return to God through Jesus, we have then also returned to our original design and our purpose—to bring others back to where we are.

Go then and make disciples of all the nations,

baptizing them in the name of the Father, the Son and of the Holy Spirit. (Matthew 28.19)

Jesus gave this command to those who would follow him. He asked of us who have received God's love to show that same love to others who do not know him. This is our design, God's will, and the end to be attained in our lives that we go and make disciples of all the nations. If God is no respecter of people, and his heart beats for us as one, then our hearts must beat as his. This is the only way we will accomplish his will.

We are a people designed, purposed, and called to accomplish God's will on this earth. What is that? To spread the gospel or good news of Jesus Christ, that all men might be saved. How do we accomplish that will? Through the gifts and talents that God gives us. When these gifts and talents are combined with God's design, they become our destiny, our calling, that thing which drives us and motivates us. Some argue that they have no talent, but there is something innate in all us that cries out for a greater, nobler purpose than simply being one of the crowd and living day to day; that says, I was born to make a difference somehow. This is the passion of our scars, the design of our lives. By this we know that our scars were not in vain, but that our lives can be turned around to accomplish good.

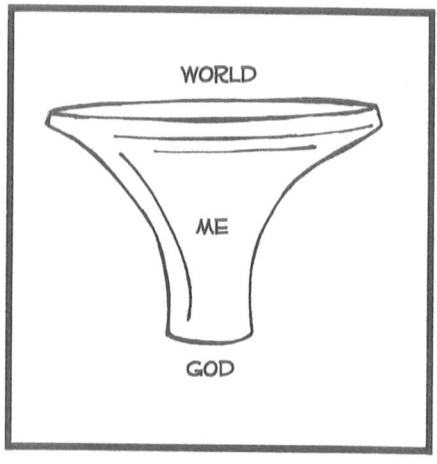

Our purpose is like this funnel. It starts off wide at the mouth as we realize the magnitude of the task at hand, the purpose to which God calls us. It has a global focus, but it decreases around the middle. Here is where we see what God has called us to specifically and what our part is in the whole design. I am always in the middle, because that's where God needs me to be—in the midst of his presence and in the midst of this world making disciples. The funnel continues to narrow down, as we are led back to the father, as we lead others back to God. Ultimately he is the end to be attained.

Friend, your life is no accident. You are not here by chance or by happenstance. If we could just see the hands that meticulously formed us, the love that wove us together in our mother's womb, the love that looked at our unformed bodies and called us beloved, we would realize how precious our lives truly are. The love poured into us is the same love that God wants us to share with others. It is this same love that becomes the driving force in our lives to make disciples of the nations. We cannot be selfish in the light of this knowledge. There are people dying every day who have not heard the name of Jesus. They have not heard that there is a God who wants to give them an abundant life, to provide for their need, heal their hurts, soothe their pains, and hold them in hands that have their names engraved on them. These people—God's lost children—will spend an eternity apart from him if they do not get a chance to hear and answer the same call we have been given. This is our destiny and our design, to accomplish God's will on this earth and lead a dying world back to their God; there can be no purpose nobler than this.

Chapter 3
HERITAGE

I am the workmanship of an original design and I have a purpose, but we cannot stop here. We must begin to move down that funnel towards the middle, because that is where we are most effective. Often time, too many of us remain at the top, saying, what difference can I make? What can one person do?

Knowing then that our destiny begins with our original design, we must take a trip back in order to continue forward. We have to know what our heritage is, our spiritual heritage. There is an old adage that reads, we must know where our fathers have been in order to know where we are going. So let's begins with our heritage.

Heritage is something transmitted by or acquired from a predecessor. We ask, "What Would Jesus Do?" when we are faced with difficult situations, but to answer that question we must know what kind of man he was (or is). We must know what he did, what he said, how he lived. This is what our spiritual heritage consists of. It's not something we see when we acquire it, but once we make it ours, it is conveyed into something we can see. Heritage then becomes glory and glory is something we see in the life of one man in particular: Joseph.

Joseph was one of the twelve sons born to the patriarch Jacob. He was still a teenager when he was sold into slavery by his brothers and taken into Egypt. There he was eventually thrown into prison on false charges and forgotten by everyone (Genesis 37-50). Though he was in a situation akin to hell, Joseph decidedly answered God's call and was moved from the prison to the palace, where he was placed in command of the nation, second only to the pharaoh. When Joseph reconciled with his brothers, he sent them back to Canaan with the message, *tell my father of all my glory in Egypt (Genesis 45.13)*. Joseph wanted his father to know that he had aspired to greatness, doing what God had called him to do through the heritage Jacob had passed onto him.

Glory is defined as a height of prosperity or achievement; something that secures praise or renown; a distinguished quality or asset. When Joseph spoke of *"all my glory"*, he was describing the tangible or material greatness he had come to: the palace, the position, the wealth, the honor, and the prestige. All of this was made possible because of the heritage left for him by his father Jacob, his grandfather Isaac, and his great-grandfather Abraham. The tangible became proof of the intangible and the heritage acquired and utilized became the glory seen.

When we look into the lives of our spiritual fathers, it is glory we seek, because glory is evidence of what they believed, received and consequently, what they did. It gives us a foundation to continue building on, even when that foundation begins in a pit. Rock bottom is a hard place to hit, but it is in this place that God can take the mess our lives have become and build a foundation that cannot be shaken. Like Joseph, we have to stop looking at the pit as a place of shame and understand that God can take even what was meant for our demise and use it to our advantage. You learn quickly that you can't fall off the bottom, you can only move up.

Joseph found himself in more than one pit in his life, but each time, he waited on God and put his heritage to work for him. He diligently strived to bring back his fathers' glory through his life and we do the same when we put our heritage to work for us. Abraham, Isaac, and Jacob were Joseph's natural fathers, but for us, these men are our spiritual fathers (Romans 4.11). When we accept Christ into our hearts, they become a part of our heritage, beginning with Abraham, the father of faith.

> *Now (in Haran) the Lord said to Abram, Go for yourself (for your advantage) away from your country, from your relatives and your father's house to the land I will show you. And I will make of you a great nation, I will bless you (with abundant increase of favors) and make your name famous and distinguished and you will be a blessing (dispensing good to others). And I will bless those who bless you (who confer prosperity or happiness upon you) and curse him who curses or uses insolent language toward you; in you will all families and kindred of the earth be blessed (and by you they will bless themselves). (Genesis 12.1–3)*

Joseph's great-grandfather was Abraham, the father of faith; but when we first meet Abraham, he is an idol worshipping, nomadic shepherd named Abram living in ancient Mesopotamia. He follows his father to Haran and claims nothing more than a loving wife and a herd of livestock. This is his life until the day God calls him and changes the direction of his life with one word, "Go". The rewards Abram reaps for his obedience are exceedingly great—

- He is blessed.
- His name is great, famous.
- He is a blessing.
- He would become a great nation.
- Blessed are those who bless him.
- Cursed are those who curse him.
- The world is and will be blessed though him.

—but beyond all that, it is credited to him that even though he doesn't know where he is going, Abram stands on God's promises and goes. These promises are the birth of a legacy he will pass onto his family, his household, and his descendants. Abram had only to obey God when he said go and continue following him. Granted, it wasn't easy at times following God, trusting him for food in a famine, protection in the midst of territorial wars, an heir from a barren wife; but as Abram proved his faith, so God proved faithful to his promises. Before he saw the fulfillment of any of it though, Abram had to pay the price to claim what was promised him.

> *Arise, walk through the land, the length of it and the breadth of it, for I will give it to you. (Genesis 13.17)*

For all that Abram received, he had only two desires for himself: children and his own parcel of land. But he had to wait a lifetime for these: a son born to him at one hundred years of age and the title deed to a burial plot. Abram would give up a life of security and comfort to wander the hillsides and pastures of Canaan at God's request. He could have easily argued that there was much he gave up, but before he could say anything, God answered him:

> *Fear not Abram, I am your shield, your abundant compensation and your reward shall be exceedingly great. (Genesis 15.1)*

I compensate your sacrifices, God told him, the very things you give up for my sake. I am your abundance. Not just a son, but a nation of sons. Not just a plot of land, but a country. Not just for you, but for future generations.

God changed his name from Abram to Abraham to prove himself. Now, whenever Abraham answered to his new name, he was answering God's call and his promises. He was not just an exalted father as the name Abram implied, but he was a father of many. Like Abraham, our sacrifices are never greater than our reward. We will never give up more than God can return to us. We need only to have the same kind of faith to believe that if God said it, he will do it. We can believe this because of the legacy that has been passed to us from Abraham. It was by faith that Abraham lived and by faith he taught his son about God; and by faith that this legacy was alive in the generations that followed.

> *By faith Abraham, when he was called, obeyed…[with eyes of] faith, Isaac, looking far into the future, invoked blessings upon Jacob and Esau. [Prompted] by faith, Jacob when he was dying, blessed each of Joseph's sons…[Actuated] by faith, Joseph, when nearing the end of his life referred to [the promise of God for] the departure of the Israelites out of Egypt… (Hebrews 11.8, 20-22)*

Because Abraham is our spiritual father, the beginning of our spiritual heritage, the same measure of faith he had now becomes ours: faith to answer when called, faith to obey when told to go, faith to believe when the circumstances seem impossible, faith to walk when we want to stop and faith to pass on that same heritage. This was the legacy Abraham left for Isaac when he died and was buried in the only piece of land he owned.

Abraham named his son whom Sarah bore to him Isaac. (Genesis 21.3)

Isaac was the child of promise, born in the land of promise to the man of faith. Some might be intimidated to have that kind of legacy to live up to, but not Isaac. Because he was surrounded by faith, it wasn't a stretch for him to live by faith. He witnessed the rewards of that lifestyle, made a decision to walk as his father did and in everything he did, he put God first. As a result his life was marked by success.

But I do not speak of success in conventional terms. Even though Isaac *became great and gained more and more until he became very wealthy and distinguished (Genesis 26.13),* he understood that these riches did not mark his success. Because of the faith that was modeled for him, Isaac understood that success was determined by obedience. Our first example of this in scripture is found after the death of Sarah, Isaac's mother. Abraham sent his servant Eliezer back to Assyria to find a wife for Isaac. His success depended on one thing: that he do what Abraham commanded.

> *Then you shall be cleared from my oath when you come to my kindred, and if they do not give her to you, you shall be free and innocent from my oath. (Genesis 24.41)*

Eliezer went back as asked. When he met Rebekkah, Abraham's niece, he gave her the marriage proposition. If she said no, he was released from his assignment. If she said yes, he was still released. Either way he found success. The key was in going. When we look at success the way Abraham and Isaac did, then we learn to look at God's role in the situation rather than what we can accomplish. Ultimately, if God has asked us to be obedient, then he will bless our efforts, as he did for Eliezer.

> *Rebekkah is before you; take her and go, and let her be the wife of your master's son. (Genesis 24.51)*

Thus, Isaac learned to be successful as his father was successful. He was ready to obey when God called in the midst of a famine and said,

> *Live in the land of which I will tell you. Dwell temporarily in this land and I will be with you, and I will favor you with blessings, for to you and your descendants I will give all these lands and I will perform the oath which I swore to Abraham your father. I will make your descendants to multiply as the stars in the sky and will give to your posterity all these lands (kingdoms) and by your Offspring shall all nations on earth be blessed, or by Him bless themselves. (Genesis 26.2-4)*

God asked him to continue living with purpose, even in a dead season. Just as Eliezer's success depended on going back and proposing marriage to Rebekkah, Isaac had only to be obedient by living in the land God brought him to and planting seed. He re-dug the wells that were established in his father's time and when he came across opposition, he dug his own well. There he took the legacy that Abraham left him and made it his own; and so, yes, *because Abraham listened to and obeyed my voice and kept my charge, my commands, my statutes and my laws (Genesis 26. 5),*

Isaac would have a part of Abraham's promises, but through his own obedience, he would secure blessing, success, and an inheritance for himself and for his children.

> *Then Isaac sowed seed in that land and received in the same year a hundred times as much as he had planted and the Lord favored him with blessings. (Genesis 26.12)*

The God of his father Abraham became the God of Isaac and in time, the God of Jacob.

> *The Lord said to her, [the founders of] two nations are in your womb, and the separation of two peoples has begun in your body; the one people shall be stronger that the other and the elder shall serve the younger. (Genesis 25.23)*

When we meet Jacob, Isaac's younger son, we meet a man obsessed with God's blessings. He listens as his grandfather Abraham recounts his travels through Canaan at the behest of this nameless God. He witnesses as the promises of God are fulfilled in his father's life and desires the same things for himself. He is unwilling to surrender his life to God though. Jacob has no time for religion. He has a blessing to acquire and will do it by any means necessary, be it a bowl of lentil soup with which to extort his brother's birthright or the hide of a goat with which to deceive Isaac into blessing him instead of his brother. After all, a divine edict favored him above Esau: *"The elder shall serve the younger"*, his mother was told.

Why did Jacob struggle so much trying to get the blessing? He lived in a society that favored the first to open a womb. Subsequent children were often relegated to the position of servant hood and Jacob desired more than that. Though he loved his brother Esau, Jacob didn't want to be subject to him and he knew that the blessing would grant him the power to transform his life.

Jacob justified his actions to get the blessing, but God could not approve of the way Jacob went about getting it. Consequently, God would not allow him to find the fulfillment of the promise as he gave it. God wanted Jacob to be occupied with the "blesser", thereby resulting in the "blessing." He wanted Jacob to surrender his life to him so that he could activate the blessing within him, the God-given power that already resided in Jacob that would allow him to change his life and the lives of those around him. After all, he was the seed of Abraham and Abraham was made a blessing so that he could be a blessing. This was Jacob's heritage, but he failed to see that he could not have one without the other. He could not have the blessing without the God who gave it.

And so Jacob struggled greatly to get what was already his. Jacob achieved riches and "success", but it was outside of God's will, bringing with it much sorrow. He traveled back to Haran and met his uncle Laban. He, too, was a schemer, using whatever means he deemed necessary for his own profit. Laban increased his riches by swindling Jacob out of twenty years of rightfully earned wages. Instead of his true love Rachel, Jacob was made drunk on his wedding day and given her sister Leah. A week later, he married Rachel and set the two sisters on a lifetime of competition, so much so that he rarely found peace at home. Though they were a sign of his strength and virility, Jacob's children proved to be a greater source of heartache in his old age.

It was in this time of anguish that God called him and said, "Go home". Jacob had no time for God when it was just him seeking the fulfillment of a prophecy, but now, having come to the end of himself and his schemes, the chosen son was left with no recourse but to return to the God of his fathers. He finally recognized the blessing he had always carried within him by recognizing the blesser.

And you shall tell my father of all my glory in Egypt and of all that you have seen. (Genesis 4.13)

We come to Joseph and find that heritage tested. He is sold for twenty pieces of silver and lead to another country, a slave. Humbled by the cruel bondage, he chooses to remember the legacy his fathers passed on to him and decidedly lives his life with purpose. He keeps the God of his fathers in the forefront of everything he does. When his master's wife tries to seduce him, he refuses her advances and answers, *"How then can I do this great evil and sin against God?" (Genesis 39.9)* Joseph uses the measure of faith Abraham passed to him to believe God had not abandoned him to die a slave, but would indeed be faithful to the promises he had given him regarding his destiny. He uses the understanding of success Isaac left him to obey and find favor in the eyes of his master. *[He] left all that he had in Joseph's charge and paid no attention to anything he had except the food he ate (Genesis 39.6).* Joseph seeks the blesser, activating the blessing within him that the glory of his fathers might become his glory. Joseph is arrayed in honor, riches and the best Egypt had to offer. He is able to change his life from slave to prince and leave a legacy and inheritance for his own sons, Ephraim, and Manasseh.

To faith, success, and blessing, he adds perseverance. In the twenty years apart from his family, Joseph has only his dreams to carry him through the seemingly hopeless situations he finds himself in. He has to learn how to persevere through humiliation, unforgiveness, false accusations and perhaps the worst circumstance of all, being forgotten. It is this measure of perseverance that takes him to his destiny, from the prison cell to the palace, to bring life during a famine.

This same measure of perseverance is passed onto to us, along with faith to believe the impossible, success through obedience and blessing to change the circumstances of our lives. The inheritance does not end there though. The list continues as we read through the Bible, with names like Moses, Boaz, Ruth, David, Josiah, Mary, and Jesus. Added to this inheritance with each name we find faithfulness, praise, humility, and integrity. We continue the list into a spiritual heritage rich with names such as Martin Luther, Saint Patrick, Dietrich Bonhoeffer, Amy Simple McPherson, Kathryn Kulman, Billy Graham, etc. Some of these names are familiar and some are not. There are hundreds and thousands more, ordinary people in the annals of history, but extraordinary because of their faith. They represent the heritage left to us, and with each name comes a different strength we can call ours because of what was bequeathed to them, received by them, and passed on to us. This great heritage, once received, *[bestows] upon us all things that [are requisite and suited] to life and godliness, through the [full, personal] knowledge of Him Who called us by and to His own glory and excellence (virtue). (2 Peter 1.3)*

By looking at our spiritual heritage, we see only what took these men and women onto their destinies. Let's peruse the natural side for a moment though—our own biological parents and forefathers. What role does this heritage play in our lives?

Our first nature is that of sin. We got it from our parents, and we will pass it on to our children. And when sin is complete, it will bring about death. This equates into eternal separation from God and counters the purpose of our spiritual heritage, which serves to strengthen us towards our destiny. There are times we can benefit from it (e.g., wealth, health, etc.). There are even times our fathers can leave us a legacy that helps us in our walk with God. The apostle Paul wrote of Timothy, a young pastor:

> *I am calling up memories of your sincere and unqualified faith (the leaning of your entire personality on God in Christ in absolute trust and confidence in His power, wisdom, and goodness), [a faith] that first lived permanently in [the heart of] your grandmother Lois and your mother Eunice and now, I am [fully] persuaded, [dwells] in you also. (2 Timothy 1.5)*

In the long run though, our natural heritage serves only to deter us from our calling. Sickness, disease and unforgiveness are inherited characteristics destroying lives instead of empowering them. Should we even take this heritage into account then? We have to; we must know where our fathers have been in order to avoid traveling down that same path. The heritage left to me was one of anger, unforgiveness and pride. It's impossible to take these things and work them into anything useful. I know, I tried. If this is the kind of legacy you are looking at, take heart, there is hope.

As stated previously, God's original design was for a family. When we accept Jesus Christ as our Lord and Savior, our creator then becomes our heavenly father and we become his children. Salvation translates into adoption and the adopted son has the same legal standing as the biological son. We become heirs to this heritage, possessing everything we need for life.

Do you know your heavenly father? Have you been adopted yet? Take a look at the heritage you've been left. It may look good, but is it complete? Is it lacking in anything? God is calling you now. He is asking you if you would like to become his child. If this is a decision you want to make right now, pray with me:

God, I want you to be my father. My life is lacking without you. I believe in the sacrifice Jesus made on the cross so that I could return to you. I receive this free gift from you as you receive me now as your child.

If you have prayed these words, rejoice. Your prayer has been heard and answered. You are now a child of God! (See Appendix A)

❧ Chapter 4 ❧
RELATIONSHIP

With original design comes a heritage that equips us to fulfill our destinies. We are now part of a covenant that provides for us and marks God's relationship with us.

Isaac accepts success because of the example his father left for him. When God tells him to stay in the land in the midst of a famine and plant seed, Isaac obeys. He returns to the wells his father dug but the local herdsmen do not want competition for water and oppose his every move. Isaac moves on twice before digging his own well of living water (Genesis 26.19). He names it Rehoboth, saying, *for now the Lord has made room for us and we shall be fruitful (Genesis 26.22)*. God then renews his covenant with Isaac.

Up until now, Isaac lived according to his father's faith. It was only when he had to go out and dig his own well that he discovered his own faith and his relationship with God became personal. The God of Abraham became the God of Isaac.

Our heritage leads us to a basic understanding of God: he is our father. He created us in his image and desires for us to fulfill our destinies. But this is just the beginning. We can approach God on the merits of what our spiritual fathers have done and receive what they received. Or we can delve in deeper and realize all God has done for us by well-digging. By personalizing our relationship with him through the covenant he's established.

In order to sustain his household, Isaac had to secure a constant source of water. He and his servants would spend days digging into the Canaanite soil to find a well. Without the well, access to water was impossible and without water, they could not live in the land. Spiritually speaking, when we start well-digging—that is, delving into our relationship with God, discovering who he is, what's he's done, getting to know him—we begin to understand that without him and his covenant, we cannot access God or all the good things he's set aside for us.

What is a covenant? It is a binding contract between two or more parties who agree on promises, stipulations, privileges and responsibilities. It is the access point between heaven and earth, between God and us, between what's been done for us and what's been promised to us.

This is the covenant God made with Abraham:

> *I will make of you a great nation, I will bless you (with abundant increase of favors) and make your name famous and distinguished and you will be a blessing (dispensing good to others). And I will bless those who bless you (who confer prosperity or happiness upon you) and curse him who curses or uses insolent language toward you; in you will all families and kindred of the earth be blessed. (Genesis 12.2)*

These are the seven promises God made to Abraham when he called him and initiated the covenant. He made the promises, determined the privileges, and meted out the responsibilities. Abraham's part was to obey, *walk and live habitually before [God] and be perfect (blameless, wholehearted, complete) (Genesis 17.1).* God's part was to provide the power to fulfill the promises he made to Abraham.

If Abraham had undertaken the task to establish the covenant, then it would have been void of power when he died. Because it was God who made the covenant, the covenant was a living one. It depended on God and not Abraham. It continues from one generation to another, including in it each subsequent generation, that God might fulfill his promise. This is why God calls them by name, the God of Abraham, Isaac, Jacob, and your forefathers. He wanted his children to know that he was alive and faithful to the promises he had made, even generations before them, that in Abraham all the people of the earth should be blessed.

> *And I [God] will establish my covenant between Me and you and your descendants after you throughout their generation for an everlasting, solemn pledge, to be a God to you and to your posterity after you. (Genesis 17.7)*

God wanted to bless all people, not just one man. His promise to Abraham was not just for a son, but a nation of sons. Jacob would receive an even greater revelation of the depths of God's love when he answered his call to destiny, that he should sire not just a nation, but a company of nations (Genesis 35.11-12).

The covenant isn't just about the promises though. God wants to bless his people, yes, but he wants to be their God foremost. He wants a personal relationship with them. God did not just want to be the God of Abraham. He wanted to be the God of Isaac and of his son Jacob and of his son Joseph and of his son Ephraim and of his son Rephah and of his descendant Joshua and of his children and of their children and eventually of the generations of children who were not of the same blood but of the same spirit. He wanted to be the God of the nations and of the company of nations counted towards Jacob. God wants to be your God and mine, and it was through this covenant that a way was made for this to be possible. Through Jesus Christ, God made it possible for all of us to be adopted as his. As the Son of God, Jesus would be born into this covenant, bringing salvation to mankind. He would bring the ultimate blessing to all the people of this world.

This covenant is our claim to God and to the heritage he gives us—the promises, the purpose, and the design. God is calling and asking if we will follow him, take our part in that promise, and allow him to be our God.

As much as it speaks to our past, our spiritual fathers and our beginning, this covenant also represents our future. It is our provision for the future as well as our connection to the past. Through the covenant, Abraham was blessed or empowered with abundant increases of wealth as God loosed his favor upon him and caused men to do the same. During Abraham's sojourner in Gerar, Sarah was wrongly taken into the harem of the king. When she was returned to Abraham:

> *Abimelech [the king] brought sheep and cattle and male and female slaves and gave them to Abraham ... to Sarah, he said, I am giving [Abraham] a thousand shekels of silver. (Genesis 20.14, 16)*

Through the covenant, this same favor is available to us, Abraham's progeny. As his spiritual children, our part of the covenant is the same as Abraham's—to obey God, to live in his presence, to be perfect, blameless, wholehearted, and complete. God in turn provides for us as he did for Isaac, Jacob and for a man called Mephibosheth, through the covenant his father made.

Mephibosheth was the son of Jonathan and the grandson of Saul, the first official king of

Israel (2 Samuel 9). He was born royalty and eventual heir to the throne, but this would not be so. He would lose his father and grandfather in a fierce battle for Israel's independence. A childhood accident would leave him maimed for life. And the kingdom that should have been his was instead given over to David, a shepherd boy! Now, instead of being known as The Prince, Mephibosheth became known as The Cripple—lame and without a future. He had nothing left to him except the one thing he refused to recognize: covenant.

This covenant was established when Jonathan and David were young men serving in the king's army. Jonathan, the heir to the throne, and David, a shepherd boy turned soldier and anointed to be king, formed a friendship extending beyond the bounds of death. However, what was more extraordinary than their relationship was their loyalty to God. David served faithfully Saul, the chosen king, though the throne was promised to him. Jonathan voluntarily stepped down as heir to serve God by serving David, his anointed one.

Jonathan stripped himself of the robe that was on him and gave it to David and his armor, even his sword, his bow and his girdle. (1 Samuel 18.4)

By giving the armor, sword, bow and girdle—all significant articles of his position and his strength—to David, Jonathan was surrendering his will and his might to him. He was humbling himself to the position of servant and armor bearer though the throne was his by right of birth. His humility would cause him to consider his house and his family before his own ambitions and welfare and was part of the legacy Jonathan would leave for Mephibosheth. He made a covenant with David to assure provision for his house, much as God's covenant with Abraham provided for his descendants.

While I am still alive you shall not only show me the loving-kindness of the Lord, so that I die not, but also you shall not cut off your kindness from my house forever...so Jonathan made a covenant with the house of David. (1 Samuel 20.14, 46)

Then Jonathan died in battle. The house of Saul was replaced with the house of David and the male heirs to Saul were executed. Those that survived lived their life in exile. Mephibosheth lived in the shadow of what should have been. He grew up and tried to forget his destiny. He could not look beyond his handicap and his lost status to draw from the well or from the covenant his father left him. He chose instead to live beneath the standards of his royal birth because he saw himself only as a dead dog (2 Samuel 9.8).

David upheld his end of the covenant for Jonathan's sake and restored to Mephibosheth his title, his lands, and his wealth. He moved him to the palace and shared his meals with him as he would his own sons. For Mephibosheth, his destiny was reflected in his name. Instead of being called The Cripple, he became known as Mephibosheth Who Eats Continually at the King's Table, all because of the covenant his father made.

∞ Chapter 5 ∞
CURSES

What does it mean to be called? It is the means to the end, the venue by which God will accomplish his purpose and his will on this earth. Yet even this definition is much too complicated. Being called simply means God is calling us by name. It means he is talking to us each day. He has made more than a general statement as to why he created us. He looks at his children corporately and says, *go make disciples of all the nations (Matthew 28.19).* And to us individually, he says, *I will instruct you and teach you in the way you should go; I will counsel you and watch over you (Psalm 32.8).* This is what it means to be called.

Here we come to a fork in the road of life we have been meandering along on. We have a choice to make, right or left. The journey is uncertain either way, but we will only reach our destiny going by the way of blessing. That road will lead us to the father who calls us. The other road, well... should we choose to take this road, we realize too late that it is "cursed."

The heritage left to me was one of anger,

bitterness and unforgiveness. For one hundred years, mother has passed this to daughter and the dysfunction has grown with each generation. Such a heritage only works towards its own end, but just as God was with Abraham, so was he with us. Growing up with my mother and my grandmother, we would often hear stories of God's provision and grace. When the cupboards were empty, no income to speak of, God would send a family friend shopping for our needs. One day, a pastor came visiting in our neighborhood. He dropped off bags of groceries, intended for someone else who wasn't home. Church members would call and ask, "What sizes are your girls? We have clothes for them."

I knew no better. To me, God was a good God, but those were only stories of things past. Hopefully, my thought was, he still provided like that. I didn't understand that with every story told, my mother was passing on our heritage, our purpose. She was preparing us for what God was calling us to do.

Because my father was absent for much of my childhood, my mother would constantly remind my siblings and I that God was our father. There wasn't a prayer we said where we did not address God as *Papa Dios* (Father God). Legacy was being established. She was preparing us for our destinies. God, she assured us, would use our talents. She didn't know to what end, but she knew these would be a part of our end. Whether she understood it or not, she was developing us to hear from God.

In Genesis, we read God's discourse with Abraham concerning the future of his descendants. Know positively, God told him:

> ... *that your descendants will be strangers, dwelling as temporary residents in a land that is not theirs, and they will be slaves and will be afflicted and oppressed for four hundred years. And in the fourth generation they [your descendants] shall come back here [to Canaan] again. (Genesis 15.13-16)*

God was preparing Abraham so he could prepare his children. After all, this was the reason he was called (Genesis 18.19). Abraham may not have understood why his descendants would be slaves, but he had God's assurance that it was only for a time. They would come out with the spoils of Egypt and would return to the land of their inheritance, no longer wanderers but masters of the house.

In 2 Samuel 7.12-13, we find another example of this preparation. God tells David that his son will be the one to build a temple for God, though it is on David's heart to do it. As we follow the story in 1 Chronicles 22.5-6, David says, *I will therefore make preparations for it…Then he called for Solomon his son and charged him to build a house for the Lord, God of Israel.* David began collecting materials for the construction before he died and in doing so, he began preparing Solomon to hear from God and to accomplish what God had called him to.

If we have no one to prepare us then this is something we must do for ourselves, by studying our heritage, reading God's word, and praying. All of these develop our hearing because they are designed to reveal God to us. They are two-part, our seeking and God responding. It then becomes our choice to walk in that knowledge—living with purpose, discovering our heritage, developing our hearing and reap God's blessings.

However, if we choose not to walk in that path, we are willfully rejecting our destiny, and if we are not walking in God's blessing, then we are walking under a curse. Curses are the opposite of blessings. They obstruct our path to prevent us from moving forward. They exist in hopes of destroying what God has called. They counter the good things God has planned for us and they are generational, continuing from father to son. Most often they come in the form of the traits and characteristics we inherit from our natural fathers.

Though anointed of God, David stepped out of God's blessings and into a curse when he committed adultery with Bathsheba, the lovely wife of his captain Uriah (2 Samuel 11 and 12). To make matters worse, David later murdered Uriah after Bathsheba announced she was pregnant. Sordid details aside, David's ultimate sin was his pride. He could have had any maiden in the kingdom. God's favor and blessing were at his disposal. And if this was not enough, God told him, he would have given him even more (2 Samuel 12.8). Instead David chose to abuse his power and position, and take what had been given to another. Consequently, he had to face the results of his actions. He would lose five of his children:

- Bathsheba's son would die a week following his birth (2 Samuel 12).
- Ammon, David's heir, would rape his half-sister Tamar and be murdered by his brother Absalom in retribution (2 Samuel 13).
- Absalom would lead a coup d'état against his father, only to be buried by him (2 Samuel 18).
- Tamar lived as a widow in her brother's house, never to come into her father's presence again (2 Samuel 13.20).
- Adonijah would lose his life in a vain attempt for the throne (1 Kings 1 and 2).

This curse infected David's family and was passed to the subsequent generations:

- Solomon reigned, but lost favor with God for allowing his foreign wives to lead him astray (1 Kings 11.1-11).
- Rehoboam, Solomon's son, lacked wisdom and the kingdom was torn from him (1 Kings 12.1-17).
- Abijam, Rehoboam's son, continued under the same curse, ignoring God's call (1 Kings 15.1-8).

From Solomon to Abijam, God's heritage and covenant was available to them to change the curse to blessing, but they chose instead to despise their destinies. They chose to allow the curse to continue. We have the freewill to choose the life we will live, blessed, or cursed. We must be aware of the consequences that follow the choices we make. They will either empower us or ruin our lives and the lives of the generations that follow.

David's children saw the punishment for their father's sin to the detriment of their own lives. Four generations were cursed by their pride. We must understand that God has only our good in mind. He wants to see us prosper (Jeremiah 29.11). He will not allow curses to run indefinitely if we are willing to seek him for the blessing. To Abraham, God set the promise for deliverance at four generations, and it is in the fourth generation we meet Asa *who did right in the eyes of the Lord, as did David his father [forefather] (1 Kings 12.11).* He saw the blessing of God come into his life because he chose to do right and walk with God. As a result of Asa's obedience to the calling on his life, the curse was broken.

I am the fourth generation, bound by the heritage of my fathers—well, my mothers. We are a family of matriarchs: me, my mother, my grandmother, my great-grandmother. We were and are strong women in our own right, in our own situations, but we are bound by one-hundred years of dysfunction, one-hundred years of mothers rejecting their children. This was my heritage, my curse. With children of my own, I have a choice to make. My calling lies before me and their futures are at stake. With the revelation of that knowledge, what do I choose?

Abraham prepared his family and his household for their destinies. He passed onto them the heritage of faith, of hearing God and seeking him. Isaac, Jacob, and Joseph followed; and as we turn the last page of Genesis to the first chapter of Exodus, we find a people waiting. Abraham, Isaac, and Jacob sired sons, but now there was a nation to contend with. Now the calling that the first received was about to be required from a generation of slaves.

These slaves knew their heritage. We are the fourth generation, they told each other. We are that generation God told our father

Abraham about. And just as time changes the circumstances of our lives, so it changes the expectancy. The awe and reverence we possess for God increases in the revelation that we are about to walk into something greater.

So the people waited as we are waiting. We see what God has done and what has been left for us by our spiritual fathers. We adhere to the covenant of our fathers and obey God. Now we wait to hear God. God, what would you have us do? We are expecting great works. What will our part be?

The clock ticks louder and there is one man in that fourth generation who finds himself under a curse, running away from his destiny and from God's call—Moses.

But before we are introduced to Moses, we meet remarkable women walking in the fullness of their destinies, imparting their heritage onto the fourth generation that will see deliverance from slavery. Before we meet Moses, we meet Shiprah and Puah.

Shiprah and Puah (Exodus 1.15-21) are midwives to the Hebrew women. They obey when called before the Pharaoh and listen as he commands them to kill the Hebrew boys they deliver. They might leave his presence grieving and anxious, or they leave indifferent to his words because of the promises made to Abraham. Cursed would be those who cursed them. Egypt would be inviting God's judgment and they would not be a part of that. Besides, Jacob's daughters were different. They delivered their children quickly. They were daughters of the promise, strong women because God gave them strength.

When Shiprah and Puah are called before the pharaoh again, they stand up and proclaim God's blessing on them—Hebrew women are not like Egyptian women. Pharaoh puts them out of his court, and they walk away rejoicing, even with the knowledge that the king would continue oppressing them. God rewards them and gives them sons of their own.

Before we are introduced to Moses, we meet Jochebed, wife of Amran (Exodus 2.1-10). At the behest of her husband, she makes a miniature ark and places her three-month-old son in it. With tears perhaps, but filled with the same faith Abraham left her, she sets the basket on the Nile and sends her daughter

Miriam to follow it. Then she goes home to wait. The babe was now in God's hands.

Still a child herself, Miriam steps out on faith. While her mother waits, she follows the ark down the banks of the river and past the fields where her people groan in labor. She follows it as it flows right into the arms of a young heathen princess, the daughter of the very man who has decreed the babe's death. Miriam gasps as the pharaoh's daughter catches eye of the basket and sends her servant to retrieve it. She holds her breath, anticipating her response and looking for the opportunity to save her brother.

And it is here, before we are introduced to Moses, that we meet Hatshepsut (1), the pharaoh's daughter. She lifts the cover of the basket and sees a fine child soundly sleeping within. Miriam runs to the princess and bows down.

"Shall I go get a wet nurse for you from among the Hebrew women," she asks, "that she might nurse your son?"

"Go," Hatshepsut says, and Miriam laughs to witness God's providence so early in her life. She rejoices as she pulls her mother along, barely able to speak. "Come get your son." Jochebed bows herself before the princess and is told, "Nurse this child for me and I will pay you wages for your work. His name shall be Moses and he shall be my son."

Jochebed rises, Miriam behind her, both barely able to contain their joy. God had multiplied it and added his reward to the house of Amram, returning the son sentenced to die.

God also blessed the house of pharaoh, of his daughter Hatshepsut, for Jochebed's sake. He had promised Abraham, blessed are those who bless you. Egypt experienced God's favor and blessing during this time. It was during her reign that the economy flourished, making Egypt the breadbasket of the world once again. She conquered her enemies, real and perceived, and extended her borders into other lands.

Hatshepsut achieved a peace that her people had not known after centuries of occupation by other nations. She did what no other woman had done in her time and accomplished what no other pharaoh had accomplished in the history of her people (2). Even though Hatshepsut was polytheistic, she was not beyond God's call. She saw her nation prosper because of her obedience and because of that, God blessed her household.

This blessing, however, does not automatically bring his approval. Moses was now the grandson of the ruling monarch who had oppressed and killed God's people. He served as a daily reminder to the pharaoh of his transgressions, a daily opportunity for him to repent of his sins.

But when he chose instead to increase the oppression of the nation of Israel, God brought his judgment on Egypt. He had promised Abraham, *I will bring judgment on that nation whom they serve, and afterward they will come out with great possessions (Genesis 15.14).*

Egypt lost God's favor by oppressing his people and killing them. What was once a place of refuge became a burial ground. Consequently, God saw fit to remove their wealth and give it to his chosen ones. He began the transfer of wealth he had promised Abraham, first to Amram and then as judgment against the house of Egypt.

As Egypt sank under the curse it had brought upon itself, Israel waited to step into her calling. While they waited, they passed on their heritage and prepared themselves for their destinies.

This is the kind of people God is looking for—a people willing to follow him and listen for him, a people ready to walk under a blessing and not a curse and a people willing to teach their children about him. For this reason was Abraham called and for the same reason were these women forever memorialized in the pages of Exodus. Shiprah and Puah watched their sons grow into men because they were willing to prepare them for God's calling. You are the fourth generation, they said, promised to see deliverance from slavery. Jochebed was to give her son to Hatshepsut at the age of four, but in the years she had him, she prepared him to hear from God. "You are God's chosen," she told him. "By his hand, he saved you. By his hand he kept you. And by his hand he will bring you back."

They could do this only because of the heritage that promised God would never leave them, that he would bless them, favor them, answer them when they called and speak when they listened. For Jochebed, when the moment came to entrust her baby in the care of Providence, she could because she had heard him say, "Trust me with his life. I will cradle him in my hand as he drifts down the river. He will sleep more contentedly than he has ever, and I will be his Savior. I will bring him to the place where he will know me, even in the house of him who seeks to destroy him."

Like Jochebed, we need to be the people God is searching for—a people willing to follow him, willing to hear him, willing to walk under a blessing and not a curse and willing to teach our children about him.

∽ Chapter 6 ∾
HOWEVER

We choose the road of blessing and walk through its gates. We develop our ears to hear God and we wait, anticipating our part in his plan. What will he say? Will I be a preacher, a prophet? Will people look at me and say, look at what God has done through her? "Lord, speak to me, I'm listening. Is anyone there? Hello?"

In developing our hearing, we find that opposition enters the picture. The circumstances we face in life are there to deafen our ears to God's voice and to distract us from his plan. Moreover, if we are distracted, we will not fulfill our destiny. We have to expect opposition. That's a difficult word to hear, but it's something that needs to be said. Opposition increases when we decide to seek after God and fulfill our purpose. We must, however, remain firm in our decision and gird ourselves up for the fight. We must learn to keep our focus on God, to rest and not sleep.

In my own life, I witnessed as the generations who preceded me despised their calling, choosing instead to walk under a curse. Even despite the mess I made of my life, God redeemed me and gave me purpose. I heard him say, I have called you, but as I waited, circumstances started adding pressure. I became pregnant again, outside of wedlock, but we were married in my second trimester. Between the hormones and the stress of life, I began slipping into depression. My heart was so heavy I couldn't see my own worth. This was not something I could easily share with others. After all, I was a Christian. Of course I was supposed to be happy, especially since my situation seemingly worked itself out and I wasn't just another statistic.

In my silence, I isolated myself to the point where I felt like I was the only person who had experienced depression. I felt like I was forgotten—alone. I could not control my anger and I would often have to apologize to the ones I loved the most.

I gave birth to a girl. Beautiful, perfect, with a head full of black curly hair, but she was a colicky baby. She cried and nothing I did comforted her. It wasn't long before I found myself crying with her.

After The Call

So they set over [the Israelites] taskmasters to afflict and oppress them with [increased] burdens. (Exodus 1.8, 11)

We must expect opposition. It came for Isaac in Gerar at the wells of his father, for Jacob when he returned to the Canaan, for Joseph when his brothers sold him into slavery, and it came for the children of Israel when pharaoh caused them to become slaves. I was no exception. No matter how distracting those situations are, though, we must remain focused. When we are faced with opposition, we must continue holding onto the promises of our fathers and cry out to the one who calls us.

However, after a long time (nearly forty years) the king of Egypt died; and the Israelites were sighing and groaning because of the bondage; they kept crying; and their cry because of slavery ascended to God. (Exodus 2.23)

Their cries ascended to the very throne room of heaven and God was prepared to answer those cries. He had a HOWEVER ready for the circumstances that sought to destroy the people he had chosen. God was not silent. He called them, spoke to them, whispered into their ears, "I hear your cries, your weeping. I hear the cracking of the whip as it strikes your back. I see the stripes where it breaks your skin. I hear you whisper, where are you God? I hear you ask, how long? I know it seems like a long time, but I've already taken care of this. I've already set my plan into motion and you will leave and never look behind you again. Just keep calling me, keep looking to me and while it seems nothing is happening, you'll turn and see the shackles have been taken off. I will sing songs of deliverance to you and hold you in my bosom. I will cover you and keep you forever. You will find that you were so distracted in me, I took care of it all. No one is there to hurt you. Only keep focused on me. You won't see the terror around you if you look to me."

We must be so focused on God that we are distracted from our distraction. This mindset does not deny the reality of our situations. On the contrary, it strengthens us to endure them and then move past them.

This is where we usually stop though. The Israelites could not look past their oppression to see God. They focused their attention on their taskmasters, instead of focusing on God and like them, we tend to do the same thing. We focus on what we can sense instead of what we know. With our natural eyes we see, but only what's around us. With our senses, we feel the oppression; we hear our own cries and wonder if anyone else has heard us. We taste our tears and wonder if they water anything but anguish. How long, Lord, how long will you make us wait? Where is the fulfillment of your promises? When will the pain stop? When will I get peace from my torments?

> *God heard their sighing and groaning… [He] saw the Israelites and took knowledge of them and concerned himself about them. (Exodus 2.24-25)*

God is listening for our cries. He is waiting for them. He concerns himself with our situations so that he can do something about them. First by distracting us from them but then he moves us to a place of promise.

Like the Israelites, we too have our land of bondage, our land of Egypt. We dwell in a place where we are ensnared by the past, by the things that once held us and sought to kill us. As long as we remain shackled to those things, we cannot move into the place that God is calling us to. We cannot move into our "secret place", our land of promise, our land of Canaan. God knows that where we chose to dwell makes a difference in what we will focus on. David chose to make his dwelling in the Lord.

> *Psalm 91.1 He who dwells in the secret place of the Most High shall remain stable and fixed under the shadow of the Almighty [Whose power no foe can withstand].*
>
> *2 I will say of the Lord, He is my Refuge and my Fortress, my God; on Him I lean and rely, and in Him I [confidently] trust!*
>
> *3 For [then] He will deliver you from the snare of the fowler and from the deadly pestilence.*
>
> *4 [Then] He will cover you with His pinions, and under His wings shall you trust and find refuge; His truth and His faithfulness are a shield and a buckler.*
>
> *5 You shall not be afraid of the terror of the night, nor of the arrow (the evil plots and slanders of the wicked) that flies by day,*
>
> *6 Nor of the pestilence that stalks in darkness, nor of the destruction and sudden death that surprise and lay waste at noonday.*
>
> *7 A thousand may fall at your side, and ten thousand at your right hand, but it shall not come near you.*
>
> *8 Only a spectator shall you be [yourself inaccessible in the secret place of the Most High] as you witness the reward of the wicked.*

9 Because you have made the Lord your refuge, and the Most High your dwelling place,

10 There shall no evil befall you, nor any plague or calamity come near your tent.

11 For He will give His angels [especial] charge over you to accompany and defend and preserve you in all your ways [of obedience and service].

12 They shall bear you up on their hands, lest you dash your foot against a stone.

13 You shall tread upon the lion and adder; the young lion and the serpent shall you trample underfoot.

14 Because he has set his love upon Me, therefore will I deliver him; I will set him on high, because he knows and understands My name [has a personal knowledge of My mercy, love, and kindness -- trusts and relies on Me, knowing I will never forsake him, no, never].

15 He shall call upon Me, and I will answer him; I will be with him in trouble, I will deliver him and honor him.

16 With long life will I satisfy him and show him My salvation.

As a man of war, David understood what it meant to be surrounded by the enemy. He knew what it was like to face opposition, even from his own family and friends.

However, when life's circumstances became grim, David knew who to turn to. He knew when you revert your attention to God and hide in him, no foe or weapon can distract you from him or from your calling.

What is your dwelling place? Are you living in Egypt when God is calling you to Canaan, saying, "Don't look at the oppression, look to my face? Don't you know that I cry when you cry? Don't you know that my heart breaks to see you hurt? I know the pain blinds you, but don't sleep, stay focused, stay alert, here with me. Look beyond what you can see. I know you are weary. Just rest in me—don't sleep, not yet."

And while we are resting in him, God is working to turn us around.

> *And they cried in a loud voice, O Lord, holy and true, how long now before you will sit in judgment and avenge those who dwell on the earth? Then they were each given a long and flowing and festive white robe and told to rest and wait patiently a little while longer... (Revelations 6.10-11)*
>
> *For this reason they are now before the very throne of God and serve him day and night in*

> *his sanctuary (temple) and he who is sitting upon the throne will protect and spread his tabernacle over and shelter them with his presence. (Revelations 7.15)*
>
> *For the lamb who is in the midst of the throne will be their shepherd and he will guide them to the springs of the waters of life; and God will wipe away every tear from their eyes. (Revelations 7.17)*

We read these verses from Revelations and find that God's answer to the tribulation saints will be to clothe them in his rest and give them patience to await the final judgment he himself will execute. God will protect them from their enemies and then he will comfort them and wipe away their tears. His answer is the same for us. We are granted God's rest and his patience that we might endure our opposition.

We must not confuse the two though—sleep and rest, that is. While in college, I received a concussion. Because the resulting injury might have been more damaging, I was told not to sleep for more than two hours at a time that night. I wanted sleep, but I had to forego my body's desire to shut down so that I was alert to any danger not detected yet. When we are tired, depressed, weary of enduring, the first thing our bodies tend to do is shut down. The result is we become dull to the dangers around us. In contrast, when we are at rest, though we are not in position to fight opposition, we are ready to go at a moment's notice. We are alert to our surroundings and to our enemies.

In God, I found the stability for the emotions that had become unbalanced in me. I was able to break beyond the depression and function with some depth of normalcy. After all, I had a household to care for. So while I cared for them, I continued waiting and listening. I began working full-time again and now instead of depression, I became overwhelmed with my responsibilities. Remember, opposition is promised. I now came to the point where I would often ask, Lord, when do I get to sleep? When will my rest come? This had become my focus. I couldn't distinguish between the two.

I became pregnant again—another daughter. Now I had three small children running around the house. Energy was all they had, and I was running on fumes. A full-time job, a husband, a family, a household to take care of... Lord, I need sleep! I get up at four in the morning to spend time with you. I stay up until ten at night to spend time with my husband. I have time for everyone but myself and all I want is sleep. I am tired, Lord.

At the end of his life here on earth, Jesus found he too was weary. He became burdened with the task ahead of him and his soul grew heavy. The only thing he knew to do was to pray. So out he went with John and Peter to the garden of Gethsemane.

> *And when he came to the place, he said to them, pray that you may not (at all) enter into temptation. (Luke 22.40)*

"Pray and be alert," he said. "Pray that you may be alert. Pray not that God might remove the temptations, but that you might be made aware of Satan's deceptions that would bring you into the temptation to sleep and lose your focus."

> *And he withdrew from them about a stone's throw and knelt down and prayed, saying, Father, if you are willing, remove this cup from me; yet not my will but always yours be done. And being in an agony of mind, he prayed all the more earnestly and intently and his sweat became like great clots of blood*

dropping down upon the ground. (Luke 22.41-42, 44)

Jesus was but a few feet from his disciples. He could see them but more so they could see him, fervent in prayer, blood and sweat streaming down his face. They could see his grief, his physical anguish. They could hear the urgency in his words as he poured out his heart to God.

Or they could have if they had been awake.

Jesus prayed and laid his heart out before God. "Father, I know there is glory on the other side of the cross. It was for this reason that I came—to die. But now the time approaches and my humanity anguishes. I don't want to die like this! I don't want to be separated from you. I don't recognize this burden weighing on me now. Father, it's your presence that I love. Don't ask me to leave that."

His prayer would have been like ours, but he kept going—<u>yet not my will but yours be done</u>. He persisted. He cried out until God distracted him from the anguish in his heart. Jesus pushed through until he was refocused on his destiny.

I ask, Lord, when do I get to sleep? When do I get to rest from these burdens? And God answers:

> *There appeared to him an angel from heaven, strengthening him in spirit. (Luke 22.43)*

God wants for us to master the situations that oppress us and the only way to do that is to go through it. We must be able to endure these situations to the end. Otherwise, these situations will master us and kill us. They are an end to themselves. They are there to oppose the very work God is doing in our lives.

Had Jesus not endured separation from God, had he not endured death, how could he then have mastered it and secured salvation for mankind? When we are able to master our opposition, we do not shrink away when the next situation arises. We are strong and confident and able move beyond it and in moving beyond it, we are able to fulfill the purpose to which we were called. Jesus turned to God all the anguish in his heart with the earnest desire to fulfill his destiny. And when the anguish drew its strength from his physical body, weakening him in the process, Jesus prayed all the more fervently.

The answer he received was spiritual strength. He received a peace and a confidence that God had everything under control.

What was the result of this "prayer meeting"? Without fear or anxiety, Jesus went off to meet the one who would accuse him. Judas, one of the twelve whom Jesus had poured himself into for three years, lead the Roman soldiers to him and betrayed him with a kiss. Jesus was scourged and beaten beyond recognition. He was mocked, crowned with a laurel of thorns, and hailed as king. A purple robe was thrown on his striped, wounded back. He was stripped naked and nailed to a cross, while the rest of his worldly possessions were gambled on at his feet. He was abandoned and forsaken. This was the longest day of his life only to end in a borrowed tomb.

Jesus prayed and received strength to endure what he went through so that we could return to our heavenly Father in right standing. It was for us that he endured all that and it brought him to the other side of the cross, an empty tomb, risen in glory, that he might draw all men to himself and bring them to God.

What about the other two, Peter and John? Jesus told them twice, pray that you may not enter at all into temptation. They slept, though, and were unprepared when the opposition came. Peter denied Jesus three times and John abandoned him. Both were powerless to fight off the temptation to save self because they had slept and not prayed.

In the midst of our heartaches, distractions, pains and humiliations, friend, I want you to be assured that God has heard your cries. He answers us by calling us and distracting us from our circumstances. He asks us to rest so he can give us strength to endure our oppression.

Never doubt that your cries are anything but precious to God. David wrote of him, *you number and record my wanderings; put my tears into your bottle - are they not in your book? (Psalm 56.8)*. God has written them down. Though he forgets our sins, he shall not forget our tears, *but shall wipe them away (Revelations 21.4)*.

⊱ Chapter 7 ⊰
COVERED UP

So, now that our ears are ready to hear, we must learn to listen. Like rest and sleep, though, we often confuse these two as well, hearing and listening. Hearing opens our ears to the possibility of receiving sound; listening involves processing that sound.

> *God saw the Israelites and took knowledge of them and concerned himself about them [knowing all, understanding, remembering all] (Exodus 2.25).*

God told Abraham that the fourth generation would be led out of slavery from Egypt and of the fourth generation there was one man who was about to realize he was about to walk into his calling—Moses.

Now Moses was a man without a sure identity. He was Hebrew by blood, but his own people did not consider him their brother. He grew up a son of Egypt, but he was not Egyptian. Moses tried to balance both worlds and be a part of both, but was unable to. He killed an Egyptian slave master beating on a Hebrew slave and was forced to go into exile. Moses traveled through the wilderness and came to Midian where he met Jethro and married Jethro's daughter, Zipporah. They had two sons. He worked for his father-in-law and kept sheep in the backside of the desert. He put his past behind him and was content to dwell where he was. Moses spent forty years in Egypt watching his people toil as slaves, while God encouraged his people with the promise of deliverance. Moses spent another forty years in Midian keeping sheep while God comforted his people, telling them, "Your deliverer comes." The obvious question here is if God had concerned himself with the plight of his children, why did he wait so long to call Moses?

Moses lived his life the way we live ours—we work, we marry, we have children and we surround ourselves with familiar things. He worked, he married, he had two sons and he became comfortable in his new life. Any material thing he had been heir to was left in Egypt, along with his destiny. Without a heritage to claim as his own, he had to struggle for success, recognition, wealth, and authority. Without a purpose, he had no reason for being. Like many of us, he had to decide what he would do and build up from there. What kind of legacy was Moses building? He was a stranger in a strange land (Exodus 2.22). Certainly, that would have been the "glory" he would have left his sons had not God met him in the wilderness one day.

> *The Angel of the Lord appeared to him in the flame of fire out of the midst of a bush; and he looked and behold, the bush burned with fire, yet was not consumed. And Moses said, I will now turn aside and see this great sight, why the bush is not burned. And when the Lord saw that he turned aside to see, God called to him out of the midst of the bush. (Exodus 3.2-4)*

This burning bush gives us a painted picture of God's glory—a burning bush that is not consumed. We've defined glory as a height of prosperity or achievement; something that secures praise or renown. A distinguished quality or asset; and like Joseph's glory, what was seen was evidence of what wasn't seen. The fire and the bush were the evidence or the representation of the God we cannot see. What God was showing Moses in the midst of that bush was the essence of who he is—glory, someone worthy of praise, honor, and respect, like the fire. Fire, by nature, destroys whatever it comes in contact with. It moves rapidly and persistently, consuming whatever lies in its path. It is brilliant, standing apart in the darkest and lowest places. *The Lord your God is a consuming fire (Deuteronomy 4.24),* Moses would later write.

The most striking characteristic of God, however, is seen in the bush itself. Though it was ablaze, it was not consumed. Fire is an awesome force to contend with, often difficult to control. Here, God shows the majesty of his glory in his restraint, and that restraint signifies his love. What do I mean? If you have ever held a newborn infant, you know how delicate that child is in your arms. You realize how much bigger and stronger you are, and you hold them gently. Your touch is not careless but calculated. You restrain how you normally act lest the child should be injured.

The Lord your God is a consuming fire.

But the bush burned with fire, yet was not consumed.

God came to Moses in a form that would show him the essence of his being and identify who it was who called him. He went one step further and showed how much greater he was by demonstrating restraint so that the bush was not consumed, and Moses was not immersed in the blaze as he approached it. This is the reason for the restraint—that we may approach him. The farther away we are from the object of our attention, the less we are focused on it. When God draws us to him, we must be able to approach him without being consumed or destroyed. This is why the first man and woman were expelled from the garden. God's glory could not abide with their sin. This is God's mercy in action. We were not able to save ourselves, so he came clothed in the flesh as Jesus Christ and offered a sacrifice he could accept, that when we received it, we could be adopted as God's children. Now having received salvation, God shows restraint, that we might approach him when he calls.

When I pick up my children from school, I call them to get their attention and they come running to me. They know that I love them, and my only intentions are for their good. There is no fear in them because of the love and time spent in them. However there are instances when I call them, and they do not answer. Usually there is some form of mischief involved along with a fear of punishment. Though I would not consume them, they do not answer.

God is the same way. He is our loving father and we must know that when he calls we should answer him and come running. Nothing should inhibit us from doing so, yet, so many things do—opposition, distractions, fear, etc. We become like Moses, creating a heritage that has no lasting value. We recognize our mortality and limitations. We look ahead and are wary of the consequences of our actions, knowing we have no control of the future. We take these failures and allow fear to take root in our hearts, "protecting" us from any pain and hurt we may experience in the future. We start wondering "what-if" until the "what-ifs" haunt us, drowning out all the other voices. Then we fail again because we have allowed fear to stop us from hearing and listening and approaching the God who calls. We fail again because instead of developing ears to hear him, we have allowed our ears to become deaf, unable to hear God calling.

Why did God wait so long to call Moses? It is easy to say God waited forty years to call Moses, but the fact is Moses wasn't listening.

Hebrew or Egyptian, without a sure identity, Moses had no purpose. He existed until his life was demanded of him for the life he took. Then he ran away—away from Egypt, away from his people, away from his heritage, away from his destiny and away from God. Fear invaded his heart—fear of being caught, fear of dying for his crime, fear of being rejected by his own brethren and fear of not knowing who he truly was. All of these things deafened the voice that called him.

While the Israelites cried out to God, Moses existed in Midian, ignoring God's call for deaf ears. While God comforted them with songs of deliverance, Moses tended sheep on Mount Horeb, listening instead to the sound of the sheep resting under the shade of a tree. While God was telling his children, here comes your deliverer, Moses gave no attention to the glory of God around him, calling him, beckoning him to listen.

What must God do at times to get our attention? In a hot, dry desert, a blazing bush is nothing out of the ordinary. But, after a second look, Moses realizes it is not consumed. There are no ashes. Not a single leaf is charred, and this is enough to grab his attention. Sometimes God has to step out and break up the order of our lives and the comfort we surround ourselves with just to get an audience with us. And so Moses stops. He watches the fire being fueled by something but not the bush. He watches the flames move in the breeze. He feels the heat of the fire and knows it's not an illusion, but what can explain it? Maybe in the whisper of the wind he hears his name called. It's nothing, he tells himself, the trauma of his youth or voices from the past. He is confused. I am content here, Moses has resolved in his heart. I want nothing more.

For forty years he didn't listen as God called him. Now he didn't have a choice but to stop and hear. Why isn't God's voice sufficient enough to sustain our attention? Why don't we respond when we first hear his voice? Why do we continue walking when we hear our name called? How many times do we walk by and miss God's glory, blazing brilliantly in our darkness? Or is it that we fear what we will hear from the mouth of God?

How often did I miss God? For over twenty years I let the fear that had invaded my heart deafen my ears to God's voice—fear of being abandoned, of not having enough or of having to fend for myself. I begged God, "Let me hear your voice!" And for all my incessant begging, I missed him. I didn't hear him calling me, saying, "Ruth, my precious, beloved child. All I could hear was the sound of my own voice drowning his out."

God calls us to reveal our purpose, not to condemn us for our past transgressions or sins we neglected to give penitence for. For forty years, Moses carried the burden of having taken a human life. For forty years, his actions weighed on him, a nagging thought in the back of his mind, even while it seemed he had his life together. Certainly, he could never return to Egypt. After all, pharaoh had signed his death warrant—a life for a life; and if pharaoh could not pardon him, why should God? But as we read the first few chapters of Exodus, we find that God makes no mention of Moses' crime. God deals righteously with us and he would deal with Moses' sin, but there was a more pressing matter on hand. There was something else God wanted to say and now that he had Moses' attention, he was not going to let this opportunity pass him by.

> *And when the Lord saw that he [Moses] turned aside to see...*

❧ Chapter 8 ❧
LOVE

God doesn't call to condemn, but to save. There is no anger or frustration in his voice, only a quiet urgency that says, "I want to talk to you. Won't you hear me?" But now God has our attention. What has been burning in his heart that he has gone to such extents to get our attention?

Do not come near; put your shoes off your feet, for the place on which you stand is holy ground. Also he said, I am the God of your father, the God of Abraham, the God of Isaac and the God of Jacob. And Moses hid his face, for he was afraid to look at God. And the Lord said, I have surely seen the affliction of my people who are in Egypt and have heard their cry because of their taskmasters and oppressors; for I know their sorrows and sufferings and trials. And I have come down to deliver them out of the hand and power of the Egyptians and to bring them up out of that land to a land, good and large, a land flowing with milk and honey, a land of plenty…Now behold the cry of the Israelites has come to me and I have also seen how the Egyptians oppress them. Come now, therefore, and I will send you to pharaoh, that you may bring forth my people, the Israelites out of Egypt. (Exodus 3.5-10)

When we stop and give God our attention, God begins revealing his heart to us. We have seen God's glory. Now he begins to reveal to us the very nature of who he is—love. It is the motivation behind the salvation he offers us—*For God so loved the world (John 3.16)*. It encompasses the purpose he gives us—*Beloved, if God loved us so [very much], we also ought to love one another (1 John 4.18)*. It is who he is—*God is love (1 John 4.8)*. God and love are inseparable and when we understand this, we understand our purpose.

Our purpose, like God, is to love and to be love. It is to do as God does and to be as he is. This is God's greatest command:

> *And you shall love the Lord your God out of and with your whole heart and out of and with all your soul (your life) and out of and with all your mind (with your faculty of thought and your moral understanding) and out of and with all your strength. This is the first and principal commandment. The second is like it and is this, You shall love your neighbor as*

yourself. There is no other commandment greater than these. (Mark 12.30-31)

Our first reaction to this though is usually the same as Moses': he hid his face (Exodus 3.6). Why? Moses knew what he was hiding in his heart. Even in the restraint that God displayed, Moses was still unable to stand in the presence of God.

So what is God's response to ours?

I am the God of your father (Exodus 3.6).

It looks so simple, so unimpressive; yet when we truly listen, we hear...

"I am God, sovereign and mighty. I called your father Abraham out of the ordinary and chose him to put my affection on. I loved him and called him my friend. He loved me and took hold of the words I put in his heart. His desire became me, and I gave him a son in his old age to delight in. Blessed would be those who blessed him. Cursed would be those who cursed him. Blessed would be all the nations because of him. His name would be great.

"I am God, the God of Isaac, the son of the promise. Blessed was he because he chose me and taught his house about me. He loved me and I him. I called him blessed and gave him double the blessing I gave his father: two sons through whom he could spend his affection on. I gave him a long, satisfying life and returned his sons to him to close his eyes as he rested with me forever.

"I am God, the God of Jacob, the child of reckoning. He contended with me and refused to let go, until I blessed him and brought him came back to his father's house in peace. I multiplied him and increased his house. From his loins came twelve sons who would become the nation of Israel and inherit the land I promised their father Abraham.

"This is the glory of your fathers and I am the God who gave them this glory. They walked, dug wells, planted seeds, re-dug wells and prepared the ground for you, the fourth generation. They did that out of obedience and love for me that I could be your God too. I brought blessing and increase to them so that I could bless and increase you.

"I am the God of Levi, of Kohath, of Amram, your fathers. I brought them to Egypt and multiplied them in every way, despite the opposition, so that they could pass on the heritage of their fathers. I loved them so that I could love you. Look at what I did for them and know that I will do even more for you. If I loved them much, I will love you all the more. If I blessed them much, I will bless you all the more, even for their sakes.

"How will you know that I love you if I don't call? How will you come if I don't draw you? How will you know I have a place set for you right here next to me? How will you know you can come and be with me? Don't you know it yet? I love you. I created you with my hands and held you before your father could see you. I knew you before you knew me. I prepared all this for you."

And until we realize what God did for our fathers and why he chose them, we will fail to understand the magnitude of his answer—*I am the God of your father.* We need to look back to our heritage and see it from this end:

> *God had us in mind and had something better and greater in view for us, so that they [these heroes and heroines of faith] should not come to perfection apart from us [before we could join them]. (Hebrews 11.40)*

Abraham never saw the fulfillment of possessing the Promised Land, but he walked the land and planted seed anyway. Because of this, we can possess the promises. Through Isaac's understanding of success, we too can receive from God provision in a time of want. And because Jacob received a greater measure of the blessing, we too are empowered to prosper and live a life of abundance.

Our spiritual heritage doesn't stop there, though. It continues through the generations with people like Joshua, Ruth, Samuel, David, Daniel, and Jesus. We read the Bible and learn what God did for them and know that God will do even more for us. More recently, we meet Smith Wigglesworth, who spent every day in prayer, fasting and study that we might understand that God still heals the sick and raises the dead. We can know the Holy Spirit and the power to live a life pleasing to God because Kathryn Kulman communed daily with him. Dietrich Bonhoeffer died in a Nazi prison after two years of incarceration to show us the cost of discipleship. The list goes on and on, illustrating the depths of God's love. These men and women of God set the foundation for our spiritual walk with him. We need to understand that everything God did for them, he did for us. He had us in mind when he poured himself into them, so that when we finally stopped and turned and listened, he could pour himself into us. He loves us because he loved them first. We do not know love until we know God's love: *this is love: not that we loved God, but that He loved us (1 John 4.10)*. We love because God first loved. This is the beginning of our purpose—love.

God reveals his love to us first because it is his remedy for all the interference, attempting to deafen our ears to his call. What does his love do? It brings us to the threshold of our secret place, the place we should be dwelling in. This is the place God is calling us to. Jesus spoke of it his last night here on earth:

> *In my Father's house are many dwelling place (homes). If it were not so, I would have told you; for I am going away to prepare a place for you. (John 14.2)*

David recognized it in his psalm:

> *He who dwells in the secret place of the Most High, shall rest in the shadow of the Almighty. (Psalm 91.1)*

This secret place is the place God has prepared for us. It is a place of rest and security, away from the distractions and the doubts. This is the place where we belong. In it, God surrounds us, while his love keeps us, and it feeds us. It hides us and distracts us, leaving undisturbed by the world around us. Yes, we still live in this world but when we are dwelling in a constant place of rest and security, the circumstances in life cannot overwhelm us.

How do we get to this place, especially if it's a secret place? First, we must understand, it's not a secret from us but for us. It's our secret place. The location has been concealed from anything that tries to steal our attention. If they cannot find us, they cannot distract us.

Secondly, we know the way already:

> *And when I go and make a place for you, I will come back again and will take you to Myself, that where I am you may be also. And to the place I am going, you know the way. (John 14.3-4)*

Jesus said, *I am the Way, and the Truth and the Life (John 14.6)*. We know the way because we know the one who has gone ahead to prepare our secret place. What should we do then but follow Jesus straight to the Father and to our secret place, our place of rest and refuge? There is nothing here to draw our attention away from God and from his call.

Chapter 9
HIS LOVE GROWS

While God is calling us and drawing us near to him, we are steadily pushing him away. Consider the irony of it. We search for that true love that will never fail us and when we are presented with it, we hide our face. "How could you love me?" I asked God. "Why would you choose me?" I was presumptuous enough to tell God whom he should love and suggest that I would know better than him. But God is not offended by our emotions or our words when they are spoken from a sincere heart—*a broken and a contrite heart ... O God, You will not despise. (Psalm 51.17)*

God understands our weaknesses, *he knows our frame, He [earnestly] remembers and imprints [on His heart] that we are dust (Psalms 103.14).* He deals with us gently, as we sift through the garbage that has attached itself to us throughout the years. God waits patiently for us to return to him.

There are times, though, that even God forgoes the subtleties of gently calling us for the bluntness of breaking in beyond the things that hold us back. *For I know the thoughts and plans that I have for you, says the Lord, thoughts and plans for welfare and peace and not for evil, to give you hope in your final outcome (Jeremiah 29.11)*. It's for our benefit that he does that, even when his approach seems less than genteel.

God called out to Moses for forty years. He set a bush on fire and drew his attention back to him. He poured out his love to Moses, whose immediate reaction was to hide his face and reject that love. God will not force us to receive his love, but he will continue calling, that his love might penetrate the barriers in our hearts. At this point, God rolls up his sleeves and reveals his heart: *for God so loved the world (John 3.16)*.

John 3.16 is probably the most quoted verse of the Bible—and perhaps the one that sums it up perfectly. When we are caught up in the vacuum of our self-centered lives, we fail to see the misery of the people around us who do not know God or his love. All that changes, though, when we begin to understand God's love. We become burdened with the fact that, even though God so loved the world, not all the world knows that he loves them. This knowledge moves us to ensure others are aware of his love. This is what he was telling Moses in Exodus 3.7-10. He was saying,

"If there was any doubt as to if I exist, or am faithful to my word or am oblivious to the cry of my children, here is my answer. I have indeed, <u>without question, truly, and undeniably</u> seen the misery of my people. I have heard them crying. I know their sorrows, sufferings, and trials, because I have made them my sorrows, sufferings, and trials. And because I have done so, I will certainly do something about it.

"I promised Abraham that in the fourth generation I would deliver his children and I will do exactly as I promised. Now, it's your turn to listen, to hear and to know. This isn't about you, Moses and what you've done. I am not concerned with what has been. I am concerned with the now and I am sending you to do something about my children's situation. You've seen their oppression, you once had a zeal for them. That's why I am reminding you, Moses—because I am sending you to them."

Moses was still hiding his face when God opened up his heart to him. He had spent forty years running from God and from his purpose. Maybe when he was younger, he thought, when he had some compassion left in him, but not now. He was comfortable. He was at a place of his own making. He had left that life back in Egypt. Why did he need reminding? This is why God had called Him for forty years.

God watched for forty years as the oppression of his people reached a breaking point. Now he was asking Moses to see them as he saw them—helpless children dying prematurely before they could realize God's salvation and enter into the Promised Land. He told Moses, "I need you to do this. They will die without knowing that I love them. As I draw you to me that you may know my love, draw them to you that you can show them my love."

Now God is asking us to see his children as he sees them. He wants for us to open our eyes and see the things that break his heart, things we have the power to change if we would only go. How many children are dying around us—not just on the other side of the world—because they don't have enough to eat? How many shelters are closing each day because there are not enough people giving to support them and the work they do? How much of our time and money can we really spare? How long does it take to make an extra meal for your neighbor? How much time does it take to help others? How much time does it to take to pray?

God has been watching for too long, while we've been hiding our faces. This is our purpose and destiny and if we are to fulfill our calling, we need to love as God loves. He has a plan ready to accomplish his will—he just needs someone to go.

ॐ Chapter 10 ॐ
WHO AM I?

We show how important something is in our lives by how much attention we give to it. How much more true is that of God? He pursues us with such fervor and persistence. He gives us the undivided attention only his love warrants. Yet I am left feeling so worthless. Why? What is it I see in the mirror? I see a short, Hispanic woman with black hair and a few gray hairs mixing in. I am a wife and mother. I am impatient often and definitely quiet. I am a happy person, most of the time. This is me, my worth summed up. Still, it's not enough.

God asked Moses to hear his heart, to feel it beat, to go and Moses gives God this response:

> *Who am I that I should go to pharaoh and bring the Israelites out of Egypt? (Exodus 3.11)*

Who am I? Hispanic? Short? Wife? Mother? Creative? Yet as descriptive as these terms are, they do not define me. What I see is not who I am. It is what God sees that specifies my worth. Who am I? I am God's beloved. I am the object of his love, the essence of his being. His love is not based on who we are, but on who he is. Because we are his children, it is who we are.

"Who am I?" Moses asks, his image reflecting within the well he draws water from. As the waters ripples, all he can see is a dark, mid-stature man who's lost everything in his life. Hebrew. Egyptian. Murderer. Fugitive. Shepherd. He cannot see that even he is not beyond God's love.

Our reflections are often distorted because of the ripples in the water. The image is not clear. Sometimes it's muddy. Sometimes we can't see it at all. We take what's reflected— the memory of what we've done—and let that define who we are. Because we are covered up with other things (fear, self-righteousness, failures, self-condemnation, and inadequate self-worth) we forget that we were created in God's image. These are the only things we see mirrored back to us. And so God reveals this to me: I must ask him who I am because I cannot see clearly right now to answer that.

God draws us to the threshold of our new dwelling, of the secret place, but we can only go so far. We hear God say we are covered up with the things that our past has held us to and then he says, *put your shoes off your feet (Exodus 3.5).* God calls us and helps us identify the things that hinder us from moving forward but in the end, it will have to be an act of <u>our</u> will, an action we initiate, to put our shoes off our feet and enter into the secret place. The choice is ours. When we are faced with that decision, standing between his glory and our existence, we are the only ones who can resolve whether or not we will enter in. What happens when we do?

> *The man and his wife were both naked and were not embarrassed or ashamed in each other's presence. (Genesis 2.25)*

The first man and his wife were created in the image of God. They dwelled in the Garden of Eden and took walks with their heavenly father. The glory of God covered their naturally naked bodies and they were able to stand in each other's presence without shame. Like the burning bush, they radiated with God's glory and burned with his design, yet were not consumed. When sin entered into the picture, their coverings changed, and

God's glory was exchanged for fear. *The eyes of them both were opened, and they knew that they were naked (Genesis 3.7).* The man told God, *I was afraid because I was naked; and I hid myself (Genesis 3.10).*

Our natural reaction seems to be to hide from God because we know the closer we draw to him, the more we are exposed and made vulnerable. And in our vulnerability, we fear being discovered, rejected, and hurt again. Yet we forget that all of this is happening in God's presence. What can happen there? What pain can we experience in his love? God only wants to cover us again in his glory. The more of his presence I experience, the more my heart is comforted and the less shame I feel in standing before my God "naked", free from fear, free from a low self-esteem, free from sin. He cannot do that, though, if we are already covered up with other things.

Ignorant or unwilling, we cannot proceed into the secret place still covered and not knowing who we are. Moses was covered up with murder, pride, self-righteousness, self-condemnation, and fear. He couldn't hear God and when God finally got his attention, Moses could not approach him.

Do not come near, God said. Put your shoes off your feet, for the place on which you stand is holy ground. (Exodus 3.5)

What made the ground holy was God's presence alone. He will not compromise his holiness for our sin, no matter how much he loves us. That is what makes Jesus' sacrifice on the cross so important. It cleanses us from our sins and restores us back into right standing with God. It is only then that we can come into his presence. When we are fully covered we can only enter in so far as to be aware. We become aware that there is something more to this life than what we are living and something more to this God who calls. He draws us, but as long as we are covered with fear and sin, we can come in no further. We have a choice to yield or to continue as we are; to shed our covering or to hide.

Consider the true nature of the secret place. If God is calling us to it, if it's a place that God has prepared for us and it is indeed under the shadow of the Almighty, then we are to dwell, abide and stay in God's presence and there's more to this place than simply enjoying God and his rewards.

⁂ Chapter 11 ⁂
THE SECRET PLACE

Why does God draw us back to this secret place? Yes, we find solace in there from the woes of this world, but there is more. It is a transformation chamber with the power to change us, equip us and make us the people God has called to accomplish his will. We no longer struggle to hear, nor do we cover our faces. We become devoted, holy as God is holy, consecrated and set aside for his purpose. But we must first enter in, uncovered and willing to let God cover us.

We stand at the threshold. We can enter in no further than being aware and God says, remove your sandals. Remove those things that inhibit you from obeying me. When we do that and yield ourselves to him, our act of obedience makes us holy.

> *For as you yielded your bodily members [and faculties] as servants to impurity and ever increasing lawlessness, so now yield your bodily members [and faculties] once for all as servants to righteousness (right being and doing) [which leads] to sanctification. (Romans 6.19)*

As God's glory covered the first man and his wife in the Garden of Eden, so God's glory will cover us. It is that glory, God's righteousness, which makes us holy. Our willingness to yield ourselves to God is the only thing he is looking for, because that implies humility on our part. Humility to admit we are not able to accomplish God's will on our own. And with that humility, we are able to be changed from what we see to what God wants us to be. How do we do that?

> *Now devote your heart and soul to seeking the Lord your God. (I Chronicles 22.19)*

Devotion, or sanctification, is the wholehearted and irrevocably giving up to God of something which may never be taken back again. It is sacred. *Every devoted thing is most holy to the Lord (Leviticus 27.28)*. Throughout the Old Testament, anything that was devoted or sanctified unto God was set aside for his use:

> *Sanctify (consecrate, set apart) to Me all the firstborn [males]; whatever is first to open the womb among the Israelites, both of man and of beast, is Mine. (Exodus 13.2)*

> *And you shall anoint Aaron and his sons and sanctify (separate) them, that they may minister to Me as priests. (Exodus 30.30)*

For his pleasure to do whatever he would:

> *Every devoted thing in Israel [everything that has been vowed to the Lord] shall be yours [the Levites]. (Numbers 18.14)*

> *But all the silver and gold and vessels of bronze and iron are consecrated to the Lord; they shall come into the treasury of the Lord. (Joshua 6.19)*

Or for destruction:

> *And the city and all that is in it shall be devoted to the Lord [for destruction]. (Joshua 6.17)*

> *No one doomed to death [under the claim of divine justice], who is to be completely destroyed from among men, shall be ransomed [from suffering the death penalty]; he shall surely be put to death. (Leviticus 27.29)*

God wants our hearts and our souls, knowing that the body will follow the one that is devoted. If my heart and my soul are yielded or devoted to seeking after God, then the body too becomes holy and available to God for his design and his purpose. When we devote ourselves to God, we become sacred. We are no longer our own but belong to God. We "transfer ownership" of our being to him, for his use and his pleasure, meaning also that we cannot take back our heart or our soul. God cannot work through a man who has not given himself up completely to him. We cannot both be in charge. God will not deny us our freewill but in order to be changed, we must choose to give God our hearts and souls and let him lead. Only then are we qualified to do his work.

Moses came to the burning bush and stopped. He listened as God revealed his purpose and his love for him. Only then did Moses answer God. *Who am I that I should go to pharaoh and bring the Israelites out of Egypt? (Exodus 3.11)* He wanted to know not just who he was, but who he was that God should ask this great deed of him. What qualified a has-been like him to do as God asked?

God answered, *"I will surely be with you. (Exodus 3.12)* You are qualified to do as I have called you because I am with you," God said. When we attempt to do things apart from

God, our biggest failure becomes the measure of our pride. We will boast in the strength of our works, power, and wisdom. We will take credit for the things that only God can do.

So before God even sends us out, he grounds us. He reminds us that we are only qualified to do the work because of his presence and power in our lives. We are equipped for the task only because of him. He took the one person that everyone else wrote off, cleaned him up and sent him out.

The only thing we can take credit for is devoting ourselves to God, nothing else. When we accept Jesus as Lord and Savior, we allow him to cleanse us of our sin, removing the things that cover us. We devote ourselves to God and God grants us his presence. With his presence, he qualifies us to do his work. Without it, we are unwilling to receive instruction from God. We are unwilling to change or to be changed and thereby, forfeit our claim to the destiny as well as the rewards he has set before us. We are not going out and doing this work pro bono. Like Abraham, we have God's promises available to us. We have a covenant of provision and desire biding its time until we walk into the fullness of who we are. And like Abraham, we have the rewards of our obedience, the compensation of all the sacrifices we willfully make to follow after God, waiting for us.

However, all of these are void if we are not willing to devote ourselves to God; if we are not willing to look beyond what we see and allow God to define us. Moses understood that for all his years of training as prince and heir of Egypt, for all his success as a general in the world's greatest army and for all his expertise as Captain of the slave labor (3), he was still unable to do as God called him to because God's presence was not with him. We must understand that as well. We are only qualified when God is with us, as he was with a priest named Joshua and a prophet named Zechariah.

> *Zechariah 3.1 Then [the guiding angel] showed me Joshua the high priest standing before the Angel of the Lord, and Satan standing at Joshua's right hand to be his adversary and to accuse him.*
> *2 And the Lord said to Satan, The Lord rebuke you, O Satan! Even the Lord, Who [now and habitually] chooses Jerusalem, rebuke you! Is not this [returned captive Joshua] a brand plucked out of the fire?*

3 Now Joshua was clothed with filthy garments and was standing before the Angel [of the Lord].

4 And He spoke to those who stood before Him, saying, Take away the filthy garments from him. And He said to [Joshua], Behold, I have caused your iniquity to pass from you, and I will clothe you with rich apparel.

5 And I [Zechariah] said, Let them put a clean turban on his head. So they put a clean turban on his head and clothed him with [rich] garments. And the Angel of the Lord stood by.

6 And the Angel of the Lord [solemnly and earnestly] protested and affirmed to Joshua, saying,

7 Thus says the Lord of hosts: If you will walk in My ways and keep My charge, then also you shall rule My house and have charge of My courts, and I will give you access [to My presence] and places to walk among these who stand here.

8 Hear now, O Joshua the high priest, you and your colleagues who [usually] sit before you -- for they are men who are a sign or omen [types of what is to come] -- for behold, I will bring forth My servant the Branch.

9 For behold, upon the stone which I have set before Joshua, upon that one stone are seven eyes or facets [the all-embracing providence of God and the sevenfold radiations of the Spirit of God]. Behold, I will carve upon it its inscription, says the Lord of hosts, and I will remove the iniquity and guilt of this land in a single day.

10 In that day, says the Lord of hosts, you shall invite each man his neighbor under his own vine and his own fig tree.

Zechariah the prophet and Joshua the High Priest stood before the Angel of the Lord, but something was wrong there. Joshua was clothed in filthy garments (sin). He had lost his standing before God and like Moses, no longer in the position he was called to. Now, standing before God and man, he found himself having to answer for that.

Yet, Joshua stood before the Angel of the Lord (the incarnate Lord of the Old Testament, the second person of the Trinity, Jesus) in his filthy garments. Such a privilege is not granted to law-breakers and sinners and we do not read anywhere else where it states that he did or said anything to merit what would be done for him. It only records that he stood. He had iniquity, sin, and failure. He had given Satan "reason" to accuse, but then he did the only thing he was capable of doing: he yielded himself to God. He stood in affirmation, as though saying, "I have sinned and failed." Joshua yielded himself to God and sought his mercy.

Because of Joshua's act of devotion, the Angel of the Lord commanded the ones who stood before him to take the filthy garments from him. He said to Joshua, *behold, I have caused your iniquity to pass from you, and I will clothe you with rich apparel (Zechariah 3.4)*. He sent the angels to minister to Joshua and he himself made Joshua righteous, thereby granting him access into God's presence. The filthy garments were removed. He was instead dressed in God's glory and righteousness and was given:

1. Rule of God's house.
2. Charge of God's courts.
3. Access to God's presence.
4. Places to walk among his attendants.

These are the privileges of the call we receive. However, they are conditional. God calls us, asks us to remove the things that inhibit us from entering and bids us to come into his presence where we can be cleansed and dressed. This act of devotion should become a way of life for us. Our destiny is for a lifetime, not just a season. As we dress ourselves in the morning, so must we choose daily to put off our filthy garments and change into God's glory. And once we're dressed, we must choose to walk in God's ways and keep his commands, especially if we are to succeed in what we have been called to do. Our calling is not just about enjoying God's presence and his rewards, but leading others back along the path we've traveled so that they too can fulfill their destinies. Like Isaac, the true measure of success is not in the outcome but in the obedience, and it is in our obedience we will receive the privileges of our calling and are guaranteed success.

Zechariah the prophet also stood before the Lord. There are two things about him though distinguishing him from his colleague. These things set a precedence for how we are to proceed in our destiny.

1. He saw.
2. He spoke.

Zechariah stood with Joshua as Joshua was cleansed of his sin, restored into right standing with God and reinstated into the ministry God had called him to. Zechariah watched as he himself, Joshua's associate (ministers unto God), was made right before

God and called *a [man] symbolic of things to come*. Why was he called that? As the Angel of the Lord removed the sin of Joshua at once, so would he remove the sin of the land in a single day—on the cross through Jesus. What God does for one, he will do for another. *God shows no partiality and is no respecter of person (Acts 10.34).*

All this takes us back to the beginning, to the promise God gave to Abraham, not just for a son, but a nation of sons. God wants to restore the lands, not just one man or one nation. When we view God's purpose from his vantage point the funnel is then turned around.

We find that Jesus is in the middle of the funnel. This is the same place we are, the place we are most effective. And while our funnel narrows down, this one broadens out to include all of God's children. We are called out of this world to see God, only to be called back in to see his children. Like Zechariah, we have to get a vision of this. He understood the magnitude of God's call for him, Joshua, and the nation of Israel as a whole. He saw God's heart and the more he saw, the more he spoke.

Then I (Zechariah) said, put a new turban on his head. So they (the angels) put a clean turban on his head and clothed him, while the angel of the Lord stood by. (Zechariah 3.5)

This was his prayer. He stood before the Angel of the Lord and prayed that Joshua be reinstated as priest. He prayed that Joshua be set aside, devoted, and made holy unto God. Zechariah spoke and saw his prayer answered. When we pray and speak as God speaks, we are telling God that we have placed worth on what he has already deemed worthy. Joshua's life was precious to God. His calling and ministry were vital to his kingdom. God deemed him worthy of redemption and Zechariah, seeing this, spoke accordingly. He deemed Joshua worthy in his own sight and spoke as God did and in Zechariah speaking, the angels acted. They immediately obeyed Zechariah's words, and why wouldn't they? Zechariah had already answered God's call and received the privileges of it. He was one already made righteous, with rule of the house, authority in God's courts, access to God's presence and possessing a place among his attendants, his angels.

Angels are called ministering spirits sent to serve those who will inherit salvation (Hebrews 1.14). Psalm 103.20 calls them *mighty ones who do His commandments, hearkening to the voice of His Word*. Angels wait for a willing vessel. They obeyed Zechariah as they would God because he spoke with the voice of God. What's more interesting here is that it was Zechariah's voice the angels immediately obeyed and not that of the Angel of the Lord's. God was content with this order because it showed Zechariah had learned to be self-sufficient in God's sufficiency. God wants his people to be able to stand on their own in his strength. He wants us to be dependent on him, but to work <u>independently</u> with the resources he has given us. Whether the angels moved when the Angel of the Lord spoke or they acted when Zechariah spoke, God's word saw completion.

Joshua yielded and was qualified. Zechariah saw and he spoke, and both became symbolic of things to come—in Christ, in you, in me.

~ Chapter 12 ~
VISION

Just as Zechariah saw, so we need to see. We need to be a people of vision. What do you see? How do you see yourself? God had to open my eyes so that I could see what was truly covering me and inhibiting me from entering into his presence. From there, I had to learn how to get past what I saw.

> *And Moses said to God, who am I, that I should go to pharaoh and bring the Israelites out of Egypt? God said, I will surely be with you; and this shall be a sign to you that I have sent you: when you have brought the people out of Egypt, you shall serve God on this mountain. (Exodus 3.11-12)*

We as God's children have a problem with vision. Like Moses we tend to look behind us and answer according to our past. God, on the other hand, looks forward and answers according to our future. We are so busy reminding God of all the things we did we fail to hear God reminding us of all the things we will be. The prophet Isaiah wrote of God:

I am God, and there is none like Me, Declaring the end and the result from the beginning, and from ancient times the things that are not yet done, saying, My counsel shall stand, and I will do all My pleasure and purpose. (Isaiah 46.9-10)

God sees the end product. When he looked at Moses, he saw a man forgiven of his sins, devoted, justified, and leading his children to the promise of their forefathers. Dietrich Bonhoeffer wrote, all are created to be what in the reality of God we are already (4). God has seen our end from our beginning. When he speaks to us about our future, our destiny, he's already seen the end and then end is what he's focused on. Our lifeline may look like this:

```
         0           40            80          120
Moses {----------- {------------ {------------}
       Birth        Exile       Purpose       Death
```

But God only sees this:

The latter part of our lives, from God's standpoint, is ours to validate the need for a rebirth, but it is this part that God forgets, wipes clean and removes from us as far as the east is from the west (Psalm 103.12). So when Moses asked, who am I? God answered with this:

```
              120            80
      Moses {-------------------- {
             Death         Purpose
```

What is it we see in the mirror? Even if our vision is 20/20, if we are looking there for our identity and qualification, we'll miss it. We need to see our life through the eyes of God so that we can see his reality.

> *When you have brought the people out of Egypt, you shall serve God on this mountain. (Exodus 3.12)*

When, <u>not if</u>, Moses answered God's call, God would bring him and the children of Israel back to this mountain where the bush burned because this was where Moses first heard God. The revelation begun there was not done. He had so much more he wanted to tell Moses. It was here that Moses had heard God and his life changed and it was there the children of Israel would hear God as well and change from a group of slaves to the nation begat by God. God is looking for that one person who will answer his call and lead their generation back to the place where they first heard God. When we see our friend, our brother, a stranger in the same place we've been before, we can reach out to them and help them back to the place where we found purpose. When I see another single mother struggling with her new calling as a mother, struggling with her self-worth, I can share God's love with her and show her how God turned my life around. This is what the call of God is about. This is the end of my destiny and what my calling is meant to accomplish.

In looking ahead, God is asking Moses first to envision his task. When we are able to see something with the eyes of our mind, we are able to achieve it, because it is already real to us. Our destiny will not be real to us until we stop looking back and start looking forward. *But Moses said to God, who am I that I should go to pharaoh and bring the Israelites out of Egypt? (Exodus 3. 11)*

BUT. That one word will stand in the way of destiny and tie the hands of the Almighty

God, fortifying the walls we've built around us. But Moses said, "Who am I?" He refuted God's claim on him as his creator. He told God, "I am unworthy to be chosen and unworthy of your love. I do not deserve what you have for me. I am not righteous, not devoted and not qualified."

Moses knew he was called to be a leader but in his youth he declared himself capable and the end result was murder. Though he had the training and the ability for the position, he lacked the authority and the power to accomplish it. When he finally opened his ears to hear, he refused to allow God to qualify him because he kept looking back to his past failures, afraid he would fail again.

"Walk in my ways," God told him. "Keep my commandments and you will have charge of my courts (the sovereign officers and advisors who are the governing power). I placed pharaoh in the position he is in. He is part of my court and accountable to me (which is why I could put you in the palace to remind pharaoh of his sin and offer him a chance to repent daily). I have set you over my courts, to act on my behalf over pharaoh, his court and his kingdom and call him to accountability. You shall rule my house and my family, the children of Israel. I am their Father and as such, I have set you as guardian over them. You shall rule over them and lead them as one with authority."

And this shall be the sign to you that I have sent you. When you have brought the people out of Egypt, you shall serve God on this mountain. (Exodus 3.12)

"Look ahead, Moses. I will bring you back to where I first revealed myself to you and give you a greater revelation of who I am. I will grant you greater access to my presence and give you a greater revelation to complete the work I've given you. I will take you deeper." Moses argued though. He offered God excuses:

And Moses said to God, behold when I come to the Israelite and say to them the God of your fathers has sent me to you, and they say to me, what is his name? What shall I say to them? (Exodus 3.13)

"I was raised Egyptian," he said. "To these people, I am no more Hebrew than this bush. I dwelled within the walls their blood, sweat and tears built. You are the God of their fathers, not mine. They won't believe I heard you. They'll ask, what is his name, if you really know him? What do I tell them? People will ask who I am and how do I show them you were more than a voice in my head, or a hallucination? Who are you? Who are you to declare me competent? What qualifies you?" We turn our doubt of "us" to doubt of "him". Moses offered every excuse he could think of and because he still wasn't listening, he offered his excuses again, hoping God would change his mind and call someone else (Exodus 4.1). Moses kept arguing until he had no argument left to give. All he had left was the truth: *send someone else to do it (Exodus 4.13 NIV)*. It was not until he spoke the truth with his mouth that Moses was set free to hear what God was saying and answer God's call to go.

God wants us to yield to him. When we are honest with him ("Lord, I'm comfortable, I'm lazy, I don't want to go") he causes us to do the things he shows us:

> *Then I will sprinkle water upon you and you shall be clean from all your uncleanness; and from all your idols. I will cleanse you, a new heart will I give you and a new spirit will I put within you and I will take away the stony heart and give you a heart of flesh. <u>And I will put my spirit within you and cause you to walk in my statutes and you shall heed my</u>*

<u>ordinances and do them</u>. (Emphasis added) (Ezekiel 36.25-27)

The only thing we have to do is surrender. God will do the rest. He will help us, empower us, and cause us to do what he has called us to do, but first we <u>must</u> get beyond the excuses and be honest with God and with ourselves. *"Lord, I don't want to do this. I don't want the responsibility and the discipline required to live this life. I can't get up any earlier, I can't sleep any later. Send someone else. That's the truth. Now, what do I do from here?"*

☙ Chapter 13 ☙
THE JOURNEY

Comfort my people...speak tenderly to Jerusalem, and proclaim to her that her hard service has been completed, that her sin has been paid for, that she has received from the Lord's hand double for all her sins. (Isaiah 40.1- 2)

Every valley shall be raised up, every mountain and hill made low; the rough ground shall become level, the rugged places a plain. And the glory of the Lord will be revealed, and all mankind together will see it. For the mouth of the Lord has spoken. (Isaiah 40.4-5)

You, who bring good tidings to Zion, go up on a high mountain. You, who bring good tidings to Jerusalem, lift up your voice with a shout, lift it up, do not be afraid; say to the towns of Judah, "here is your God!" (Isaiah 40.9)

So do not fear, for I am with you; do not be dismayed, for I am your God. I will strengthen you and help you; I will uphold you with my righteous right hand. (Isaiah 41.10)

I am the Lord; that is my name! I will not give my glory to another or my praise to idols. (Isaiah 42.8)

I will pour water on the thirsty land, and streams on the dry ground; I will pour out my spirit on your offspring, and my blessing on your descendants. (Isaiah 44.3)

One will say, `I belong to the Lord'; another will call himself by the name of Jacob; still another will write on his hand, `the Lord's,' and will take the name Israel. (Isaiah 44.5)

Chapter 14
I WILL NOT LET YOU GO

"God, you and I have come to a stalemate. Words are inadequate in describing the desperation I feel. I cannot go back to what I was, neither can I proceed further. I have stopped at the threshold of the secret place. It's 1:19 AM. I sit here unable to rest, while my family sleeps. God, I'm tired of the rhetoric and the guilt. I don't know what else to do but sit here and wait. I won't let go, but I can't go on without something to show for it. If you don't do something, I'll die here."

And Jacob was left alone, and a Man wrestled with him until daybreak. And when [the Man] saw that He did not prevail against [Jacob], He touched the hollow of his thigh; and Jacob's thigh was put out of joint as he wrestled with Him. But Jacob said, I will not let you go unless you declare a blessing upon me. The man asked him, what is your name? [And in shock of realization, whispering] he said, Jacob (supplanter, schemer, trickster, swindler). And he said, your name shall no more be called Jacob, but Israel (contender with God) for you have contended and have power with God and with men and have prevailed. Then Jacob asked Him, Tell me, I pray You, what [in contrast] is Your name? But He said, Why is it that you ask My name? And [the Angel of God declared] a blessing on [Jacob] there. (Genesis 32.24-29)

Jacob packed up his household after living with Laban for decades, and traveled back to Canaan. He was returning to a father he had not seen since duping him into blessing him instead of his brother, but more so, he was returning to a brother he had swindled out of his inheritance. The last he had heard from Esau was, *"the days of mourning for my father are very near. When [he is gone] I will kill my brother Jacob." (Genesis 27.41)*

Fear became Jacob's companion as he and his household traveled through the land and came to the brook of Jabbok. Fear woke him up in the middle of the night in a cold sweat and prompted him to send his family to safety. In this moment of fear, as Jacob cried out, "Meet me or I die," God obliged him. This was Jacob's burning bush. For too long he ignored the voice of God calling him. Now God had his attention and he was going to draw him into the secret place and change him into the man he had destined him to be.

Jacob was a man chosen for the purpose of passing on Abraham's promised blessings, but he was covered in fear and arrogance. He desired God's blessings without God, and this made him deaf to God's voice and blind to his love. Everything Jacob experienced (theft, duplicity, fear, exile, etc.) was purposed to bring him back to God, remove every excuse and leave him with no recourse but to cry out to God.

And so God met him there at the brook of Jabbok and we read that the two wrestled with each other. Dawn began to break, and God fought to leave. Jacob spent what energy he had left to cry out, "BLESS ME, or it will all have been in vain." The angel of the Lord spoke and changed his name (like he did with Abraham) that he might become who he was destined to be.

"What is your name?" the angel of the Lord asked, but this question was not for his benefit. It was for Jacob's. Jacob had to see who he truly was. He had to see the things that covered him that he might remove them; otherwise he would not be able to enter into the secret place and change.

Jacob answered, "Jacob." But God said, "No, not anymore."

> *Your name shall no more be called Jacob, but Israel (contender with God) for you have contended and have power with God and men and have prevailed.*

God was calling Jacob to prepare him for his destiny and the purpose to which he was born. He was calling him to give him his true identity and his calling, but, like Moses, Jacob could only answer by what he saw—Jacob, a deceiving, supplanting, second-born conman, struggling to achieve what God had promised him. He could not see beyond his own reflection to see the God who only saw him only as Israel, a prince and successful contender with God and man.

Jacob could not see who he was, but he did understand this: when you are standing at the threshold of holiness, it's either do or die. When you've gotten a glimpse of the glory beyond, you can't turn back. There's nothing there for you. And now with the knowledge of who we truly are, all the opposition we've faced seems worse. We can't go back, and we can't go forward. So we cry out to God and something happens, a change within occurs.

When we devote ourselves to God, God grants us entrance into the secret place where we encounter the power (the blessing) to change our lives and move beyond what we see to what God sees. Only then are we able to get into the position where achieving our destiny is possible. But first we must reach the point where, like Jacob, we have exhausted every scheme and excuse.

And so Jacob spoke, *"Declare a blessing on me."*

After struggling for a century to acquire the blessing, Jacob finally realized that God was his only source. He had received the blessing of the firstborn as the second-born from his father, only to realize that this was not enough. He would still struggle for the things that were promised him. Now he faced his own burning bush and he had no one to cry out to except God. The only way he would be able to change his circumstances was if he allowed God to change him.

"Bless me," he cried, as his leg wretched out of joint. He took hold of the Angel and was unwilling to let go, lest the Angel should leave, and Jacob's struggled in vain. "My life is being demanded of me," he said. "Everything I've done is being called into accounting. I've got nothing left to lose, except if I let you go. You called me and brought me to this place. You chose me to contend with. I am Jacob, conman. That's who you called, but I am sick of it. I'm tired of being guilty. I'm tired of running after things I can't catch. I'm tired of struggling. So, if you want me to let you go, bless me. Speak words over me that will change me. Bless me. Tell me your name."

The Angel had asked Jacob his name. Now Jacob wanted to know the name of the Angel. In asking for that name, Jacob was expressing his desire to know God. He understood that within the name was the nature of the being. Jacob existed over one hundred years with the appellation of a con man, swindler, schemer, and thief. Now his name was changed to Israel, prince, contender, and victor.

"What is your name?"

"Unworthy."

"No, you are my beloved."

"How can I be? I'm not good enough. Look at what I've done."

"I only see what you are…my beloved."

And no matter how often I answer "unworthy", the answer comes back the same—Beloved. God persists because he knows that his love is strong enough to break down every wall we have constructed around us, like an army breaching the walls of a fortified city. God continues his siege of love until we surrender and are stripped before him, but it is not to ridicule, humiliate or hurt us. God wants to remove the chains that have held us back for so long. He desires to clothes us with garments of splendor and cover us with his radiant glory. He is besieging the city, not to destroy us, but to free us.

Like Jacob, God desires for us to know him and to ask him what his name is. Moses was unwilling to ask for the blessing because of how unworthy he felt. His contentment lead to complacency and the only response he could give God was, not me. He had given up on himself, but God persisted even when Moses argued. He continued until Moses was willing to be honest with him. Only then was he able to enter into the secret place where God bestowed the power to change.

God met both Jacob and Moses in the form that would attract their attention and hold it. He came to each man in such a way that they could be successful in their encounter, yet he showed them that he was still God. He disabled Jacob during the wrestling match and he restraint his glory so that Moses was not consumed when he approached. Each man left changed and proceeded in their calling according to who they were.

Sometimes we recognize a change in ourselves, not knowing when the change occurred, just knowing that it did. But for me, recognizing my true worth, I can place a time and date. I lay my head down that morning at 4:24 am. Quietly, I crawled into bed next to my husband as he turned over and put his arm around me, still asleep. In that moment I understood what God had been telling me. My husband chose me for intimacy, love, and companionship. I finally understood that through a simple act, a habit in fact that he would drape his arm around me as he slept. It wasn't in anything specific that I did or could do. He chose me because of his heart and because of his love for me. Just as God loved me, called me, and chose me to be his beloved, his child, his companion, and his delight. I understood then that it was nothing

I did. It wasn't in my perception of worth. That would never change the value God placed on me. My struggle was done.

❧ Chapter 15 ❧
OBEDIENCE

God conferred the blessing on Jacob, but it was another five years before he reconfirmed his covenant with him. Why so much time? Surely Jacob had learned by now and was listening, right? Whether or not Jacob could hear God is not the question here. Jacob lacked the one thing God needed to fully work through him to accomplish his will and place him in his destiny—obedience.

In Genesis 31, God asked Jacob to return to the land of his fathers. He even sent Esau to guide him back, but instead of following his brother to Hebron, Jacob turned towards Shechem, a small town in the opposite direction. We could reason that since he was still in Canaan, he did as God had asked, but Jacob knew better. Abraham was allowed to settle his household in Hebron. It was there in Hebron Isaac still resided and Esau had set up his tent. Hebron was the place of community and alliances and the place God was calling him to. By going to Shechem, Jacob put himself in a situation that God never intended him to be in. He allowed the fear that had been his companion for so long drive him to disobedience and then to justify his sin, setting precedence for those who would follow.

Moses was not much different. With his father-in-law's approval, Moses put his family on donkeys and set out for the land he had fled from forty years earlier.

> *Along the way at a resting place the Lord met Moses and sought to kill him (made him acutely and almost fatally ill). Now apparently he had failed to circumcise one of his sons, his wife being opposed to it, but seeing his life in such danger) Zipporah took a flint knife and cut off the foreskin of her son and cast it to touch Moses feet and said, surely you are a husband of blood to me! When He let Moses alone to recover, Zipporah said, a husband of blood you are because of the circumcision. (Exodus 4.24-26)*

This is a strange word to read. The God who had relentlessly pursued him for forty years and had called him out of the wilderness, was now trying to kill him? What we don't see here is that despite Moses' battle with his self-worth, he knew who he was. He knew his original design, his heritage, his purpose as a Hebrew and his calling. Moses lived with his natural family for the first three months of his life. He would have been circumcised (the physical sign of God's covenant with Abraham and with his posterity) on the eighth day according to Jewish tradition. Moses was covered under this covenant. By not circumcising his son, Moses showed he was not willing to devote himself or his household—that is, until he was called into accounting, just as Jacob was.

Both Jacob and Moses had to experience tragedy before completely surrendering to God. Jacob lost control of his household and Moses nearly lost his life. Sadly, these tragedies could have been averted. They could have saved themselves the heartache they experienced by simply obeying God. However costly, God allowed them their mistakes to bring them to that point of submission. At what cost do we continue holding on to the things God tells us to let go of? Is it worth the price we pay not to be obedient?

You are either obedient or you are not, there is no in-between. Jacob came to Shechem and spread out his tent. He bought property and built his house there. He attempted to settle his home outside of God's will, still purporting to be obedient. He had forgotten his request – *God, if you would bring me back to my father's house in peace, then you shall be my God.*

It's amazing how accommodating God is at times. He gave Jacob what he asked for so that he could become Jacob's God, but Jacob reneged on his promise and justified his disobedience. "I'm back in Canaan," he reasoned with himself as he turned towards Shechem, oblivious that God would send Esau—the brother who had comforted himself with thoughts of murder—to bring him home. What was the price he paid?

Through four wives, Jacob sired thirteen children, only one of which was a girl. Her name was Dinah and she was her father's daughter. For a century, Jacob pursued the one thing he thought he lacked and that led him places God never intended him to be. Dinah followed in the footsteps of her father and paid the price of her disobedience with her innocence.

In Genesis 35, we read that Dinah went to Shechem to visit the daughters of the land, she went in search of female companionship. Friends, peers, girls who were close to her age and could identify with the struggles of teenage life. After all, she reasoned with herself, her brother's wives were much too old for her and her mother just didn't understand her. It doesn't matter that her friends were pagans and did not worship the true God of her fathers, she needed them.

Dinah sought her father's permission, but Jacob denied her request. "Wait until later when I can send one of the boys to go with you," he said. But Dinah didn't want to wait. She disobeyed her father and went out on her own. The prince of the land saw her and had her forcibly brought to his house. He flirted with her and made suggestions but when she refused him, he raped her. To add insult to injury, the prince then found his heart taken with the girl and he determined to seek Jacob's permission to marry her. Dinah waited three long days in the house of her attacker, while her future lay in the balance.

Then we read that her father grieved. As often as I had read this passage, it always puzzled me why Jacob did nothing about the rape of his daughter. As a parent, the first reaction in a situation like this is usually a violent one, but the Bible only records that Jacob grieved. He understood that it was <u>his</u> disobedience that had been modeled for Dinah to imitate. It was his disobedience to God that had paved the way for this tragedy to occur. Jacob grieved because he didn't know what else to do. How could he expect others to obey when he had disobeyed?

In the days that followed, Jacob watched his family come unhinged: his sons committed murder for their sister's honor believing Jacob was impotent in defending her, and the divide between himself and his children grew wider. Jacob grieved, yes, but now he was broken to the point where he could hear God and obey. He cleansed his household and returned to the God of his father. He returned to the place of Bethel (God's house) where he first heard God. He was completely obedient, wholeheartedly devoted, broken and surrendered.

God doesn't expect us to eventually "get" what he tells us. While it learning to trust someone is a gradual process, when God says go, he expects us to go. Though Jacob could not know God had turned Esau's heart back to his brother, he had to trust a way had been made for him to return to his father's house in peace. God left no room in his plans for Jacob to go to Shechem. He was asking Jacob to trust that his deception had been forgiven, that God's love was all he needed, and that Jacob's worth was not tied up in how he felt or what he did. This was a lesson Moses learned too…the hard way.

Although he carried the sign of God's covenant with Abraham on his body, Moses chose to forget that. He was content to dwell with Jethro, and Jethro was pleased to give him his daughter Zipporah as his wife. Now as the first born of seven daughters, she had a natural inclination to lead and to take control:

> *[Now apparently he had failed to circumcise one of his sons, his wife being opposed to it… (Exodus 4.25)*

Like his wife, Moses was also a natural leader and because of this, he was confident enough to lay down the household rules: his sons would be circumcised. As a Midianite though, Zipporah was offended by the practice. Twice she called Moses a husband of blood because of it (Exodus 4.25, 26). Although he was firm with the circumcision of their first son, he began laxing in his authority and forgetting the God of his fathers. The more Zipporah voiced her opposition, the easier it became for him to give in to her desires, letting her take up the headship of the family and of the house.

Then God got his attention and set him on the path to destiny. There was a problem though: Moses had neglected the very thing that had set him apart and in that had neglected God. We cannot continue halfheartedly and accomplish what God has called us to. Moses had to take up his role as head of his household. How could he lead a nation if he could not lead his family?

So he obeyed, he reasoned with himself, as he put his sons and his wife on donkeys and set off for Egypt. Moses traveled through the desert back to the place God was calling him to, but the further they went, the sicker he got. When the fever had taken over his body, they were forced to stop at an inn and wait. Within hours, Moses was on his deathbed. But now he was broken enough to hear God and obey. In between dying breaths, he turned to Zipporah and said, "Circumcise the boy." She obeyed, understanding that his life depended on it, and in that moment, an exchange was made. Moses' household came into order. He became singly devoted to God and qualified to carry the mantle of leader to God's children.

We must understand it's not enough to go if we are not singly devoted.

Chapter 16
ESAU AND AARON

In the darkness of the twilight hours, in the solitude of my dining room where I sit, reading and studying, I see something I had not seen before—it's not just me God is calling. As God was calling Jacob home to his father's house, he was calling Esau to bring his brother home. He had changed Esau's heart back to Jacob:

Esau ran to meet him and embraced him and fell on his neck and kissed him and they wept. (Genesis 33.4)

As God was calling Moses to lead his people out of bondage, he was calling Aaron to bring him back to Egypt. The son sentenced to die is again returned to his awaiting family:

The Lord told Aaron, go into the desert to meet Moses. So he met Moses at the mountain of God and kissed him. (Exodus 4.27)

God's call is for all people, and as he works to prepare one, so is he working to prepare the other. This is where the similarities end though—our callings are as individual as we are unique, and what God requires of one, he may not of the next. Jacob and Moses would become famous in annals of history, but it would only possible because of Esau and Aaron. Though we may be in a position of low esteem, little recognition or no glory, we must realize that our destinies are integral to the plan of God, inasmuch as it propels us forward, not just for our sakes but for our brothers' as well. Their success depends on us, our success depends on them. We are two links on a chain. Together we are strong, apart we are fruitless.

As one of six children, there were times I strongly disliked one of my siblings, but I had no problem defending them because of our blood ties. I may not have liked them or their behavior at that point, but I still loved them and still acted on their behalf. Because the same father has adopted us, we are now a family, regardless of blood, race, or color. We are brothers and sisters. We need to have a love for one another that moves us to act in each other's best interest. We should build one another up and encourage one another without envy.

This is where vision comes in. We have to be able to see the bigger picture, the Great

Commission. That is our part put together with the part of others who are walking in their destinies. We have to make space when space is needed, have an encouraging word when assurance is needed and have a shoulder ready when nothing, but our silence is necessary. We must be ready to lead our brother back when they fall away and rejoice with them when they are blessed. We are our brother's keeper and as much as they depend on us, we depend on them. Had it not been for the two destined to work from the shadows, Jacob and Moses would not have found the success they did.

We yield ourselves to God and experience more opposition, but because we continue yielding, we find that God's voice becomes clearer and more defined from the other voices that seek to distract us. Where we once struggled to hear God call, our struggle now becomes one of obedience to what we have heard him say, but even that dissipates with time as we continue yielding. It is in this process, these daily experiences we find ourselves in a position to help our brothers or to be helped by them.

Jacob's favorite wife Rachel died in childbirth as they traveled back to Hebron, back to the place of community and alliances. His household set up camp in Ephrath because his grief was so great but his sojourner there was brief: Jacob could no longer stay away from God. He had come to the place where everything was meaningless if he could not completely obey the one who called him. So he picked up his tent and went home to find solace and encouragement in Esau. And though he was not chosen of God for the purpose of passing on Abraham's blessing, Esau discovered he had not been forgotten and his life was just as precious as Jacob's. He knew God's love, and this gave him peace enough to hold up his younger brother.

Moses nearly lost his life for his disobedience, but he too came to the point where all things were pointless if he was not in God's complete will. Because of Aaron's obedience, Moses became confident enough to speak on his own and declare God's word. Through Aaron's encouragement and support, Moses was able to lead God's people out of Egypt and through the desert, even when the very people he was called to lead become unleadable. Aaron was rewarded for his humility with the priesthood of God. He was exalted before the nation, as God's chosen, though he would always remain subject to his younger brother.

I have come full circle. Do I know specifically what I am called to do? Not as I first write this, but I continue yielding, my path becoming clearer with every word I write. I see as God sees and my heart is burdened for all who do not know God's purpose, his call, or his heart. I am like Esau and Aaron, called to bring my brother home.

Chapter 17
BLESSING

God changes the order of things set from the beginning, carved from tradition, just to show the infinite wisdom in the sometimes-baffling decisions he makes. God does not favor one's wealth, position, or birth. We esteem the firstborn as the beginning of our strength and God chooses the younger child, the murderer, the con man, the adulterer, the cripple to show us if they can overcome obstacles and break beyond generational curses to rise up to greatness, then so can we. Jacob's mother Rebekkah struggled to conceive for twenty years only to discover that once she did, she was carrying twins. When she inquired of the Lord, he told her, "The elder will serve the younger, Esau will serve Jacob, Edom (the nation descent from Esau) will serve Israel (the nation descent from Jacob)." Jacob would receive the blessing of the firstborn and Esau would get what was left over. What was this coveted blessing Jacob was willing to deceive his father for and Esau was willing to kill over? Before we answer that, we have one more illustration to look at.

There is a purpose in all the words that precede these and that is to change the order of our lives from merely existing to achieving our God-given destiny and to go from answering God's call to walking in it. We are to devote ourselves to God, our hearts, and souls. The heart alludes to the spirit, the soul to the sinful nature, the flesh. When the spirit is devoted unto God, it is given precedence over our flesh. Our spirit is that part of us that is in direct contact with God, but because we are sinful creatures in a sinful world, it is our flesh, the firstborn, that takes charge.

> *But [it is] not the spiritual life which came first, but the physical and then the spiritual. (1 Corinthians 15.46)*

The flesh takes prominence in the same way that Esau and Aaron had prominence as the firstborn sons. The spiritual side, the second born and younger "sibling" is then subject to the flesh much as Jacob and Moses were. But when we are reborn as God's children, a struggle is set into play as the spirit steps up to his role as leader. He is elevated above the flesh, which has been made subject to the spirit. This is where the blessings of the firstborn and the younger come in. Isaac's blessing to Jacob was:

May God give you the dew of the heavens and of the fatness of the earth and abundance of grain and new wine. Let peoples serve you and nations bow down to you; be master over your brothers and let your mother's sons bow down to you. Let everyone be cursed who curses you and favored with blessings who blesses you. (Genesis 27.28-29)

These words carried with them prophetic promises, much like the promises that God gave to Abraham. Jacob knew that when his father spoke of the fat of the land being his, he would be able to command his destiny, never to concern himself with lack. Master over his brother? Esau would serve him and his children after him. Jacob would never have to subject himself nor bow down to another. He would rise as a dominant and influential nation, honored above all the other nations of the world. Peoples and nations would be cursed or blessed dependent on how they treated him.

This was Jacob's blessing, and this is the blessing the flesh seeks because then he is subject to only his whim. He doesn't have to rise at four in the morning to spend time with a God he cannot see. He doesn't have to discipline himself or walk by faith. He doesn't have to love others, or live with purpose. He has only to concern himself with him.

The spirit, on the other hand, considers the whole man. He loves others, disciplines, and devotes himself, walks by faith and gives ear to the God who created him. This was something we saw in Jonathan's life. He denounced his position as prince and heir because he understood that he was not called to lead as his father had done. Yet he was called to serve the next in succession and though he died prematurely, his son Mephibosheth benefited from his actions. Jonathan had his posterity in mind when he served David, just as the spirit has the complete man in mind when he leads. This is because of where he comes from:

> *Then the Lord God formed man of the dust of the ground and breathed into his nostrils the breath or spirit of life; and man became a living being. (Genesis 2.7)*

When we allow our spirits to lead, we begin reflecting the image of God. We begin walking in love and in purpose and in doing so, we fulfill the destiny appointed to us. And this is possible because of what end we live towards. Are we living for our own gain or for God's? Esau wanted the blessing because it meant his father's house and favor. He went after it because it was "his" right as the firstborn. Though misguided at first, Jacob sought the blessing in fulfillment of what God had spoken over him. And they are not the only examples of this transposition:

- Isaac was chosen over his half-brother Ishmael, the son Abraham fathered with the Egyptian bond-slave Hagar, whose jealousy caused him to be exiled from the family.
- Jacob's fourth son Judah was chosen over Reuben the firstborn, who defiled his father's bed, presumptuously assuming that he would receive the blessing just because he was the firstborn.
- David was chosen over his older brothers to be king because he knew his God was bigger than a Philistine giant and he had the courage to prove it.
- David's oldest living son, Adonijah, vainly tried to ascend a throne he thought was rightfully his, yet it was Solomon the youngest son who was

chosen, because he desired God's wisdom above the riches of the world.

Jacob received the blessing of the firstborn, as the youngest, but this created havoc in the household. Esau cried out with a bitter voice and begged his father to bless even him.

Your blessing and dwelling shall all come from the fruitfulness of the earth and from the dew of the heavens above; by the sword you shall live and serve your brother. But the time shall come when you will grow restive and break loose and you shall tear his yoke off your neck. (Genesis 27.39-40)

This is the blessing Esau received. He would serve his brother and to be subject to him. He would work the land and live by it, but eventually he would grow restless and attempt to rise up from under the yoke his brother has put on him. The flesh is not content with his "little" blessing. He wants the fullness of the earth, not just the fruitfulness. He desires to be served, not to serve. He wants to see his brother bow down to him and not to bow down. The flesh is not content to see the younger one blessed with "his" blessing. The fact is he is not content to see his brother blessed at all.

> *Now Miriam and Aaron talked against Moses their brother because of his Cushite wife, for he had married a Cushite woman. And they said, has the Lord indeed spoken only by Moses? Has he not spoken also by us? And the Lord heard it. (Number 12.1-2)*

Years following the burning bush, we see a vastly different man from the one we first met in the desert. Here, Moses is called the most humble man on earth. He had come to know his worth in God after seeking God's face, dwelling in God's presence, and experiencing God's favor. It was God's love that changed him and eventually distracted him from the gossip around him. Moses didn't hear it, but the Lord did.

While the text is not specific about what became of Zipporah, Jewish historian Josephus offers his respected viewpoint on the matter. Moses, as a young prince of Egypt, married an Ethiopian princess named Tharbis (5). At the time, she was nothing more than a token bride, the spoils of a victory deserved. Yet she loved him and followed after him into the desert despite forty years of separation. Whatever the case was, we find Moses with another wife, a helpmeet, a companion in the position God had called him to.

But wait... she's black! She is a Cushite, an African woman with dark skin, kinky hair and features that are different. She's not one of them and certainly isn't chosen like they are. She's a heathen!

Miriam and Aaron used her ethnicity as an excuse to slander their brother. They were envious of his blessing. After all, they said, has not God also spoken by us?

When we seek God's face, like Moses did, and dwell in his presence and experience his love, we find that we have a powerful advocate in God. He will preserve what he has worked to produce in us. God had called Miriam and Aaron to lead in their respective ministries (prophetess and priest) but he had placed them under Moses' leadership. There they would remain, subject to the baby brother that had been twice sentenced to die and twice redeemed by their actions, Miriam at the palace and Aaron in the wilderness.

Though it seeks to overthrow the rule of the spirit, the flesh assists us in fulfilling our destiny. The flesh is comprised of our will and it is that will that sets us apart from the rest of God's creation. We are not dependent on instincts to decide what we will do or to excuse our poor decisions. We have volition, freewill, the ability to choose. We can choose to obey God, or we can choose not to. The flesh must be subject to the spirit in order to work in harmony towards the fulfillment of God's will and our destiny. Each of us has a part to play and it is up to us to yield and therein find satisfaction in the position God has called us to.

Chapter 18
CONCLUSION: WELLS LEFT UNDUG

This path we are on now is worn, neglected even. It's not appealing, nor is it inviting. It's lined with heartaches, oppression, and affliction. And this, God says, is the path to life, to destiny. Oftentimes though, we choose the other roads, the ones lined with roses and cardboard smiles, where conflicts do not exist, and we are not opposed at every turn. These are the roads we choose, even knowing we will never reach our destiny. The former is a hard road to travel, while the latter brings us to a place of "what-if's" and "if-only's". We hit another bump in the road and begin to wonder if we have chosen wisely.

When Abraham sent Eliezer to Haran to find a wife for Isaac, he made him promise not to take Isaac back there, no matter how bad the situation got. He understood that for all the things he had yet to receive from God, the past had nothing for him. It was a grave waiting to rob him of life and waiting to rob the world of blessing. He understood that once you've walked into your destiny, you can't turn back, stop up your wells or ignore them. Abraham learned that his blessing lay before him, not behind him and if he was to achieve his destiny, he was going to have to continue looking forward.

As hard as it is to push through affliction, we have to do so with the realization we have a bright future ahead of us. The wells we've tapped into look small, but beneath the surface lies a reservoir of power and blessing left to those willing to follow after God. They are springs of living water available to those ready to dig, but we must remain focused on the task. We must be prepared for the work. If we look back, we will lose sight of that which we are striving for, and once we've lost sight of it, we've lost our claim to it.

Even though their forefathers prepared them for their deliverance, the children of Israel would fail in their calling. They would continue looking back to the lives they once lived before they answered God's call. Every obstacle they encountered only drew their attention back to Egypt. Even after the miracle of the parting of the Red Sea:

> *the whole congregation of Israel murmured against Moses and Aaron in the wilderness*

and said to them, would that we had died by the hand of the Lord in Egypt, when we sat by flesh pots and ate bread to the full (Exodus 16.2-3).

In the months that followed, the children of Israel murmured at every unexpected bump in the road. This murmuring became so great it ignited God's anger. How long would they test him? If he parted the Red Sea, could he not protect them in the wilderness? If he could bring water from a rock, could he not also feed them? God would have destroyed them had it not been for Moses. Still they continued looking back and complaining until they finally had to eat their words:

As I live, says the Lord, what you have said in my hearing I will do to you: your dead bodies shall fall in the wilderness. (Numbers 14.28-29)

Abraham's blessings should have ended there. Clearly, the fourth generation had failed and would not enter the Promised Land. But someone had to take possession of the land. God had already declared it and he cannot lie. Someone had to take possession of the land and that someone was the fifth generation. The calling that the fourth generation had rejected now fell to their children.

> *But your little ones, whom you said would be prey, them will I bring in, and they shall know the land which you have despised. (Numbers 14.31)*

God had told Abraham his descendants would inherit the land and though the fourth generation was the one called to do it, it would be the fifth generation that would accomplish the task. They were reminded of the legacy left to them and then as God called their fathers, so he called them and asked them to pick up where their natural fathers had left off. God raised up a generation of conquerors who had a double calling to fulfill—their own and that of their fathers. They had a greater destiny to take possession of the land God promised their fathers and through their obedience they would receive double the reward. This was only in their going. <u>Someone had to take possession of the land.</u> Because the fourth generation would not, the fifth generation had to.

Even now, someone has to take possession. Will that be you? Abraham's promises still await you. Put yourself in the picture:

- You are blessed with everything you need to live, prosper, and enjoy life as God created us to.
- Your name is great as Abraham's was great because God is pleased to reward you for your faith.
- You are a blessing to others, that they may know God's love and return to him.
- You beget a supernatural family through those you bring back to the Father.
- Blessed are those who bless you.
- Cursed are those who curse you.
- All the peoples of this world are blessed because of you and through you and your destiny.

If we choose to reject these promises as our own, then we need to remember, it is our loss, not God's. Someone else will receive a double blessing because we chose to reject it by looking back. The choice is ours: either we take possession of the land and reap the rewards of our obedience, or we do as the fourth generations did and we reject our destiny. We have to be like Jonathan who completed what was required of him, though his death was premature. Mephibosheth did not have to pick up any part of Jonathan's calling, he had only to walk in the provision made for him through his father's covenant with David and fulfill his own calling to sit at the king's table.

What is the legacy you will leave your children? Will you walk into your destiny, that they may delight in the honor and glory God is pleased to give you? Or even knowing what you know now, is something from your past still holding you back? The choice is before you. Will you stop now and go back? Or will you walk forward into your destiny? When we come to know God and accept him as our father and God, we are adopted into a legacy greater than any man could give us. We are given a destiny, an end to strive towards, but it's also the by-product. What's different now?

I have pondered these thoughts lately, what I would have been had it not been for you, Lord. I've never spoken them nor written them, fearful they would manifest or that others would think less of me. I've been accused of hiding the truth, of living my life for you simply to cover up a past sin, or a current inadequacy; and while I know that my peace is real, what do I do with this, all these pages and notes? Are they mine to keep or do I share them? Something is different now and I cannot keep that to myself. So, having come this far, what do you say Lord? I'm listening.

And it all starts again: what is my calling? How will I accomplish your will? What have I been made to do? I pick up my pen and listen. That is the best part, I think: hearing, listening. It comes easier now. I begin writing again: *as a toddler I ran into the corner of a coffee table…*

"There will come a time when you believe everything is finished: that will be the beginning."
Louis L'Amour

After The Call

Ruth E. Griffin

APPENDIX A

[All] are justified and made upright and in right standing with God, freely and gratuitously by His grace (His unmerited favor and mercy), through the redemption which is [provided] in Christ Jesus. (Romans 3.24)

Having prayed and asked for salvation, what now? What is this right standing that we are made into? Right standing is our position in God: it means we are now sons and daughters through adoption. This is what Christianity is about—a personal relationship with God through Jesus Christ. It's not about regulations, traditions, or "this is what you have to do now". It's not about "do's" and "don'ts". Your "don'ts" are between you and God. The only "do" I will give you is this—get to know him. How? Find a good church home, a Bible-believing, Bible-teaching church that will nourish your spirit and feed your soul, somewhere you can learn about God. Spend time with him in prayer—you speaking and God listening, and then God speaking and you listening. That's the simplicity of it—it's a conversation with God. Read the Bible, become acquainted with his purpose, given to us in written form. It is our manual for living.

Ruth E. Griffin

NOTES

(1) Argubright, John. <u>Bible Believers Archaeology, Volume 1. Historical Evidence That Proves the Bible.</u> [Book On-line] (Florida: Xulon Press, 1997. Accessed August 2001) <http: biblehistory.net>

(2) Seawright, Carolyn. <u>Hatshepsut, Female Pharaoh of Egypt.</u> (Tour Egypt, 1999. Accessed August 2001) <http://www.touregypt.net/historicalessays/hatshepsut.htm>

(3) Whiston, William. Ed. [Translator] <u>Josephus, The Complete Works</u>. (Nashville: Thomas Nelson Publishers, year), p. 80.

(4) Dietrich Bonhoeffer. <u>The Cost of Discipleship.</u> (New York: A Touchstone Book, Simon & Schuster), p.79.

(5) Whiston. <u>Josephus</u>, p. 81.

Ruth E. Griffin

Acknowledgements

I would like to thank the following people for helping me along this journey. Your friendship, support, encouragement, teaching, and inspiration were, and are, invaluable. Mo, Javin, Hannah and Samantha Griffin. Pastor Chris and Jill Berkebile. Bishop Joby and Pastor Sheryl Brady. Deanna Manley. Jason, Tiffany, Kati, Noah, and Judah Speake. James Gill. Thank you!

Ruth E. Griffin

About the Author

Ruth E. Griffin could draw pictures before she could put sentences together. Eventually, though, she figured out how to do both and is now the author of several books (fiction and non-fiction) which center on women's experiences. She still designs but focuses all her free time on writing. Ruth currently lives in North Carolina with her husband and Three adult children. Her work is available at major online bookstores, while new book release and event information can be found at www.ruthegriffin.com. Email her at ruthegriffin@outlook.com.

Ruth E. Griffin

www.ingramcontent.com/pod-product-compliance
Lightning Source LLC
Chambersburg PA
CBHW021105080526
4458JCB000108/389